D0045178

ANCHOR MAN

HOW A FATHER CAN ANCHOR HIS FAMILY
IN CHRIST FOR THE NEXT 100 YEARS

STEVE FARRAR

THOMAS NELSON PUBLISHERS
Nashville

Published in Nashville, Tennessee, by Thomas Nelson, Inc.

Published in association with the literary agency of Alive Communications, 1465 Kelly Johnson Blvd., Suite #320, Colorado Springs, CO 80920.

Unless otherwise noted, Scripture quotations are from the NEW AMERICAN STANDARD BIBLE ®. Copyright © The Lockman Foundation 1960, 1962, 1963, 1968, 1971, 1972, 1973, 1975, 1977. Used by permission.

Scripture quotations noted NKJV are from THE NEW KING JAMES VERSION. Copyright © 1979, 1980, 1982, Thomas Nelson, Inc., Publishers.

Scripture quotations noted NLT are from the *Holy Bible,* New Living Translation, © 1996. Used by permission of Tyndale House Publishers, Inc., Wheaton, Illinois 60189. All rights reserved.

Library of Congress Cataloging-in-Publication Data

Farrar, Steve.
    Anchor man / Steve Farrar.
        p. cm.
    Includes bibliographical references.
    ISBN 0-7852-7308-5
    1. Fathers—Religious life. 2. Fatherhood—Religious aspects—
Christianity. I. Title.
BV4529.F37   1997
248.8'421—dc21
                                                        97–13282
                                                        CIP

Printed in the United States of America.

2 3 4 5 6 — 03 02 01 00 99 98

To

my three teenagers,
Rachel,
John,
and
Josh.

Thanks for all of the joy that the three of you have brought into the life of your mother and me.

"I have no greater joy than this,
to hear of my children walking in the truth."
3 John 4

CONTENTS

ACKNOWLEDGMENTS

It takes approximately nine months for a man to become a father. It is ironic that I have spent the last nine months researching and writing this book about fathering. There are some significant people who have helped me along the way:

- Thanks to my father, Jim Farrar, for showing me what a Christian father looks like. And to my mom, Beverly Farrar, for being the perfect complement to him for fifty years! Together, they are quite a team and still going strong.
- Thanks to my wife, Mary, for her love, patience, wisdom, and willingness to read the many drafts that came out of my printer. Her insights, as always, are invaluable to me. I always encourage single guys to outmarry themselves. That's what I did, and I continue to be a deliriously happy camper.
- Thanks to Byron Williamson for the dinner in Denver that led to this book becoming a reality. And to Rolf Zettersten, who does a tremendous job leading the troops at Thomas Nelson. It has been my pleasure to work with his excellent team.
- Vic Oliver is an editorial legend, and I have enjoyed immensely his wise counsel in shaping this manuscript. He kept me out of a couple of literary sand traps, and for that I am deeply grateful. Brian Hampton is a careful and thoughtful craftsman who jumped swiftly and

wholeheartedly into this project. Your input was more valuable than you will ever know.

- Greg Johnson and Rick Christian have gone the second and third miles in seeing this book come to completion. You guys are servants! And that's a pretty rare commodity these days.

- Dr. Dean Gage has done a superb job in freeing me from the details that accompany our conference ministry to men around the nation. Dean's expertise enabled me to give my full concentration to *Anchor Man*. Thanks, Dean. This one wouldn't have happened without your sterling efforts.

—1—

ANCHORING THE FAMILY CHAIN

"Make no little plans; they have no magic to stir men's blood."

—Daniel H. Burnham

Dennis Rodman and Howard Stern have a lot in common.

- They are both famous.
- They are both rich.
- They are both profane.
- They are both rebellious.
- They are both rude.
- They are both national role models.
- They both appear in public dressed as women.

So what's the explanation for these two adolescents who are trapped in the bodies of men? The explanation for both of them is their father.

Dennis Rodman has not seen his father in thirty years. His father now lives in the Philippines and has two wives. By those two wives he has fifteen children. But over the years he has fathered a total of twenty-seven children. According to a recent statement in *Newsweek*, Philander Rodman Jr. stated his life goal: "I'm shooting for 30."[1]

Here's a man who hasn't seen one of his sons for thirty years but has set a goal to father thirty children. That certainly helps to explain Dennis Rodman. But what about Howard Stern?

In a recent interview with *Rolling Stone,* Stern let his guard down:

> I will never have a lot of self-esteem. I don't feel very good about myself . . . I still have an inferiority complex. The way I was raised my father was always telling me I was a piece of [expletive], I think I'll go to my grave not feeling very positive about myself or that I'm very, very special. My mother used to tell me how special I was. Every time I hear my mother's voice going, "You are the most special little boy in the world," I hear my father going, "You [expletive, expletive], you are nothing but a piece of [expletive]."[2]

Can you imagine a father talking to a child like that? Now I know why Stern talks to millions of people every day on the radio like that.

Why did Howard Stern's father talk to him like that? I think that Howard's father talked to him like that because when his father was a young boy *his* father talked to him like that. In other words the problem of degrading young boys with poisoned speech in the Stern family probably didn't begin with Howard's father. And it may not have started with his father. It's entirely possible that kind of speech to children has been in the Stern family for generations.

And what about Philander Rodman? Do you think that Dennis Rodman's father came from a home where he saw his father being faithful to his mother? I can't prove this because I don't have access to the Rodman family genealogy, but I don't think it's too far off the mark to assume that the reason Dennis Rodman hasn't seen his father for thirty years is that *his* father wasn't used to seeing his father.

Proverbs 20:7 gets to the heart of the matter: "A righteous man who walks in his integrity— / How *blessed* are his sons after him" (emphasis added). Fathers with integrity don't label their children with profane names. And they don't abandon one wife to marry two more.

Rodman and Stern have a lot of money and a lot of fame. But they are not *blessed* men. And the reason they are not *blessed,* according to Proverbs, is that they had very deficient fathers.

Dennis Rodman and Howard Stern are to be pitied. And the reason they are to be pitied is that they both come from a certain type of family. Both Rodman and Stern come from what I call "drifting families."

What is a "drifting family"? Well, it's pretty simple. A "drifting family" is a family without an anchor. The father is the anchor of the family. And when fathers leave or when fathers continually degrade their wives and children, the family begins to drift. When a family begins to drift because it has lost its anchor, it can quickly begin to produce children who are insecure, self-conscious, emotionally starved, and without a moral compass.

YOUR FAMILY CHAIN

Anchors are important. They put them on ships for a reason.

A while back I read a short story about a guy who was sailing with his girlfriend across the Pacific. Several years prior he had literally sailed away from his wife and children. In the meantime he had found a woman who had also left her family. Both of them had created huge relational storms in their families. Spouses were thrown overboard and children were left to fend for themselves while these two pursued their personal happiness by sailing off into the sunset.

They were having a wonderful time sailing across the Pacific on his thirty-two-foot boat. Until the typhoon hit.

They were anchored just one hundred yards off a small, inhabited tract of land in the Marshall Islands when it hit. They knew from listening to the radio that the typhoon was coming, but it appeared that the center of the typhoon would actually pass about one hundred miles to the north. Unfortunately, the typhoon took a swift turn and suddenly this couple's safe haven was shattered, literally, by winds that were over ninety knots. They thought they would be safe because they had set two anchors, plus they had a third emergency anchor as a backup. They figured they could just batten down the hatches, make some coffee, and securely ride out the storm in the small lagoon that they had anchored in. They were wrong.

They were hit full force by the storm. The anchors gave way, they were pulled out to sea, and the towering waves began to systematically dismantle their craft. They were without anchors and they were without a rudder. They were drifting. And the drifting eventually cost the woman her life.

That couple would have been just fine if they had been on the USS *Dwight D. Eisenhower*. The *Eisenhower* is one of the largest ships in the world. This gigantic aircraft carrier is, from keel to mast, the size of a twenty-two-story building. It has a flight deck that comprises four and one-half acres. It weighs 95,000 tons. It carries over 6,000 sailors and serves those sailors 18,000 meals every day. The USS *Eisenhower* is a floating city. Oh, there's one other thing. It also has two anchors.

The *Eisenhower* anchors each weigh 60,000 pounds. Each anchor is attached to a chain that weighs 665,000 pounds and stretches to a full length of 1,082 feet. Just one solitary link in that huge chain weighs 365 pounds.

Every ship has an anchor. That anchor is at the end of a very long series of individual steel links. Each link is joined to another link. And if you trace those links one by one you'll eventually get to the anchor. It's the anchor that keeps a ship from drifting. It's the anchor that keeps the ship exactly where it needs to be.

That's the way families are. Every family is one link in a very long chain that stretches out for hundreds and even thousands of years. This chain is so long that it is hard to grasp the enormity of it. For most of us, we are doing pretty well if we are familiar with the two or three links in the chain that have come immediately before our link.

God knows the importance of family chains because He invented the family chain. *And that's why God puts such importance on each father successfully anchoring his link in the family chain.* I'm responsible to take care of my link, and you are responsible to take care of yours. That's what He wants us to do. And He wants us to do it well. There's no doubt that's what He wanted the men of Israel to do. And God used Moses to tell it to the men of Israel straight.

In Deuteronomy 6, the people of Israel are getting ready to go into the promised land after forty years of wandering in the wilderness. They have before them an absolutely unbelievable opportunity. And that opportunity is to go into the promised land, obey the laws of God, and establish a new civilization and a new culture for their children and all of the generations to come.

Not too many people have the opportunity to start a new civilization. But that's exactly what God was giving to Israel after forty years of wandering in the wilderness. God gave them a shot at starting over and doing it right. What a monumental opportunity! What an incredible calling!

And the responsibility for this new opportunity for the nation of Israel is laid squarely on the shoulders of the men. To be more specific, it is laid on the shoulders of the *fathers*.

> **Now this is the commandment, the statutes and the judgments which the LORD your God has commanded me to teach you, that you might do them in the land where you are going over to possess it, *so that you and your son and your grandson* might fear the LORD your God, to keep all His statutes and His commandments, which I command you, all the days of your life, and that your days may be prolonged.** (Deut. 6:1–2, emphasis added)

It was Ralph W. Sockman who said, "What makes greatness is starting something that will live after you." God gives every father the opportunity to do something great. And it is the wise man who makes the most of the opportunity.

If you are a father, what will live after you is your children. And then one day they will have children. And then those children will have children. What we're talking about here is a genealogy.

What is the most boring part of the Bible? What sections of the Bible are guaranteed to put a red-blooded, American Christian man to sleep faster than any other section of the Bible? Hands down, it's the genealogies. What could be more boring than reading a biblical genealogy at six in the morning?

Let me offer you something to chew on. Genealogies aren't boring. They are fascinating. If Fed Ex were to deliver by 10:30 tomorrow morning your family genealogy for the last fifteen hundred years, I guarantee you that you would be up until 10:30 the next morning poring over it. Genealogies aren't boring. What's boring is reading someone else's genealogy.

Genealogies are in the Bible for a reason. *And when you dig into them,* they are anything but boring. The reason that genealogies are so fascinating is that genealogies contain the secret of having a significant and meaningful life. Let me bottom-line this. A genealogy is nothing but a long list of guys who were sons and then eventually became fathers. So what is a genealogy? A genealogy is a lineup card. A *very* long lineup card.

Before every major-league baseball game, the managers meet at home plate and give the umpires their lineup cards. The manager lets the opposing manager and the umpires know who's going to be playing what position and he also let's them know in what order they will be batting.

A genealogy is a lineup card of fathers. And here's the scoop on every father who is in the genealogical lineup. Either he anchored his family or he didn't.

Generally speaking, if a father anchors his family in Christ, then the odds go up dramatically that his sons will anchor their families. But when he decides he knows better than God and starts living to please only himself, that's when a family begins to drift. America has millions of families that are drifting. Why are they drifting? They are drifting because they have no anchor.

When God changes a nation and brings revival, one of the primary things He does is to get ahold of some fathers and turn them into anchors. And in our day of crisis, in our day of a fatherless America, that's precisely what God is up to. God knows who His men are. He knows where they are and He knows who they are. And He knows how to strongly support them.

YOUR ASSIGNMENT, IF YOU CHOOSE TO ACCEPT IT

As I read God's instructions to the fathers of Israel in Deuteronomy 6, something struck me. *God expects each*

father to anchor his family for at least one hundred years.
No kidding. The phrase "you and your son and your grandson," when you think about it, covers right at a hundred
years. God wants His men to take their fathering so seriously
that it will anchor their families for at least a century.

You may be thinking, *I won't have a family in one hundred years*. Think again, my friend. You'll have a family in
one hundred years. You just won't be around to know them.
But they will know about you. Although you won't know
them, the way you live your life today and from here on out
will directly affect them. Very few men understand this concept. But it's a secret that God has revealed to those who love
Him. And it's an investment you can make that can pay dividends for hundreds of years after your death.

You love your wife. I love mine. You love your kids and
so do I. At this point in my life, I don't have grandchildren.
I expect that one day I will. You may not be a granddad right
now. One day you probably will be. Now read this next sen-
tence slowly. *One day your children will have grandchildren*.
Those grandchildren of your children will be four generations removed from you. They will show up about one hundred years from now, give or take ten or twenty years. Now
let me ask you a question. When was the last time you ever
thought about those kids? Maybe the better question is, Have
you ever thought about those kids?

God doesn't expect us just to take care of our families today.
*He wants your leadership to be so noble that it will carry
your family for at least a solid century*. Maybe two. Look
at the verse again:

> **Now this is the commandment, the statutes and the judg-
> ments which the LORD your God has commanded me to
> teach you, that you might do them in the land where you
> are going over to possess it, *so that you and your son and
> your grandson* might fear the LORD your God, to keep all**

**His statutes and His commandments, which I command
you, all the days of your life, and that your days may be
prolonged."** (Deut. 6:1–2, emphasis added)

The key phrase is "so that you and your son and your grand-son might fear the LORD." When you put a pencil to this, the time frame involved for those three links in the generational chain comes out somewhere in the neighborhood of one hundred to 150 years.

You may be thinking, *Wait a minute! How in the world am I ever going to do that? I've got enough on my plate right now. I've got an incredibly demanding job. I leave home early and get home late. I try to get to all my kid's games, plus I try to coach when I can. My problem is there just aren't enough hours in the day. And now you're telling me God wants me to lead my family for the next one hundred years? I'm not sure I can do it for the next one hundred days.*

I've got some good news for you. God knows that you're stretched. He sees your work and your effort to lead and provide for your family. He is not a God who makes unreasonable demands on a man. His yoke is easy and His burden is light. God doesn't ask fathers to do something that they can't do. On the contrary, He is simply asking you to do something that you can do. Only most guys don't know that they can. The great thing about leading your family for the next one hundred years is that it doesn't take any more of your time than it does to lead your family today.

Let me show you how this works. Let's take a hypothetical father who was part of Israel when Moses wrote Deuteronomy. He's a typical guy with a wife and kids. Let's call him Joe Israel.

JOE ISRAEL

Joe Israel is just a basic guy. He's a hard worker. He wants to provide for his wife and kids. Joe has a lot on his plate. When he falls into bed every night, he's tired. So how does a guy like Joe Israel lead his family for the next one hundred years?

What God wants Joe Israel to do is to be a righteous man. He wants Joe Israel to be an obedient man. He wants Joe Israel to fear and revere Him. He doesn't want Joe Israel to live one way at the office and another at home. He doesn't want Joe Israel to act one way on the way to church and another at church. He wants Joe Israel to follow Him with his whole heart.

When Joe Israel follows God with everything that he has, his son sees this. His son knows that there is nothing more important to his father than loving God. And because his father loves God, his father loves his mother, his father loves Joe Israel Jr., and he loves Joe Jr.'s brothers and sisters. Joe Jr. has friends who don't have dads because their dads have moved not to the Philippines, but to the Philistines. Joe Jr. has friends whose dads constantly degrade them and put them down. As Joe Jr. looks around at his friends, he realizes that he has the best dad around. And as he gets older, it becomes more and more clear to him that the reason his father is such a great father is that God is at the center of his life.

Time goes by and Joe Israel Jr. grows up and marries a very fine girl by the name of Rebekah Levi. It's not long before Joe Israel III comes along. Joe Israel III is a great kid who loves being with his dad. And he loves to go over to his grandfather's house. Joe Israel III is a pretty lucky kid. Not only does he have a great dad, he has a grandfather who is off the charts. As he gets older, he sees some of his friends become deeply wounded when their fathers divorce their mothers. Joe Israel III realizes how fortunate he is to have a father and a grandfather who would never divorce their wives. As Joe Israel III continues to mature, he realizes that the reason he is so blessed by a great father and a wonderful grandfather is that God is at the center of their lives. God is number one in the Israel family. And not only does he have a grand-father who is anchored on the God of Israel, he has a father who is anchored as well.

Joe Israel III is sad when his grandfather dies, but he knows that one day he will be with him forever in heaven. Even when his grandfather is gone, he doesn't drift. And the rea-son he doesn't drift is that he has a father who is still anchored. And that's why when Joe Israel III becomes a father, he will be anchored on God as well. And because he is anchored, his children will not be part of a drifting family.

Do you see how God intends Deuteronomy 6 to work? When Joe Israel dies, his godly influence lives on in the lives of his son and grandson, whom he has taught to fear the Lord. Even as Joe Israel Sr. is dying, Joe Israel III is instill-ing the same love for God into his children that he learned from his father and ultimately from his grandfather. Joe Israel III is teaching Joe Israel IV what it means to be a godly man. Even after he dies, Joe Israel Sr. is still anchoring his fam-ily because he walked with God daily. That's how a man leads his family for one hundred years.

As you read through the Bible, something begins to become very clear about God. God loves to pour out His favor on a man whose heart is fully set on following the Lord. I mean *fully* set. A guy like Joe Israel. Or a guy like you.

God wants to work in your family just as He worked in Joe Israel's family. *But,* you may be thinking, *my family chain doesn't look like that. I'm the first guy in my family to come to Christ. I don't have a father and grandfather who have passed down a godly example.*

Then you get to be the first.

You get to be the guy who puts a new link in your family chain.

I have a very good friend who pastors one of the largest churches in the United States. He influences thousands of people every week for Christ. But he's the first in his family to come to Christ. His father wasn't a Christian, his grandfather wasn't a Christian, his great-grandfather wasn't a Christian. He's the first generation in his family to follow Christ. And he can trace his family back for numerous generations. His children are the second generation to follow Christ.

He didn't have a rich, spiritual legacy of a godly father and grandfather. Spiritually speaking, his family has drifted for generations. But now his drifting family is anchored in Christ because God reached down and grabbed him when he was in high school. And the drifting of the generations came to a halt. Maybe that's what God is doing with you in your family. Abraham Lincoln said it best: "What's important is not who my ancestors were. What's important is what my children and grandchildren will become."

Are you serious about following Christ? It doesn't matter if you're the tenth Christian father in your generation or the first. The question is, "Today, are you following Christ with your whole heart?"

God loves to pour out His favor upon a man like that. And the word *bless,* which is sometimes overused in church circles, means "favor." When God blesses a man He gives great favor to that man. But here's something about God that is absolutely wild—God will not only bless that man, but God is so great and so gracious and so generous that He will bless that man's children. Even after the man dies! And not only will He bless his kids, but He will then bless their kids! All because of a guy who lived three generations prior who fully followed the Lord.

It's called compound interest.

WHY COMPOUND INTEREST SHOULD HAVE YOUR INTEREST

Compound interest is a wonderful financial principle that most of us discover too late in life. But once you understand the compound principle you can do a lot with very little. Most of us could come up with $2.74 a day. We could probably find that much in our pockets.

Ron Blue explains compound interest by demonstrating that if a guy committed to saving just $2.74 a day until he hit sixty-five, and he was able to get 12½ percent compound interest on his money, in forty years that $2.74 per day would turn into $1 million.[3] That's a nice chunk of change. And it's the result of interest that compounds and gains momentum with each passing year. At a certain point, the interest starts going crazy.

So how does a father put away spiritual principal that can begin to earn *spiritual* compound interest?

Let me answer that by asking you a question. What's the difference between a home that has a Christian father and a home that has a father who is not a Christian but has very strong "family values"? Isn't it enough just to have "family values"? No, it isn't. The father who is committed to "family values" without being committed to Christ is bankrupt. He just doesn't know it.

Ray Stedman explained it brilliantly:

> I have been in homes where there is no testimony to God or recognition of him at all. And yet they have been orderly homes, moral homes, loving homes—a joy to be in—and

where the children are obviously well adjusted and able to cope with life. Some people are ready to say, "What difference, then, does Christianity add?"

The answer is that if you investigate a home like that you will find that just a generation or so back there has been a significant Christian exposure somewhere in that family. In other words, secular homes of that character are living on the capital of faith which has been invested by a previous generation. They are spending the bank account of spiritual understanding that was set up by their recent ancestors. And in a sense, this is what our whole nation has been doing. We have been living on the spiritual bank account of our forefathers. But now the resources upon which we as a people have been drawing are gone.[4]

There's the family chain. And someone is living off the spiritual capital of a man who anchored his family a generation or two back.

Spiritual capital is the result of obedience. You put some away every day, every week, every month. As time goes by it builds. Like most investments, it builds very slowly. But there is a point after twenty or so years that the interest begins to take off. And every year to follow brings an even greater return, because the interest is starting to resemble a bullet train running at full throttle.

How do you affect your family for the next one hundred years? *By doing something today.* By being obedient today. And then by doing something tomorrow. And one day those small deposits will begin to add up. Every time you love your wife as Christ loved the church, every time you live with your wife in an understanding way, every time you grant your wife honor as fellow heir of the grace of life, you are putting away principal. It's like money in the bank.

Every time you take the time to listen to one of your kids, every time you bow your head and ask God to lead you and your family for the day, every time you refuse to alter your expense account to pick up a few extra bucks, every time you pray for a guy who stabbed you in the back in order to get a job promotion that should have gone to you, God sees those actions. And He will reward those actions.

In other words, every time you obey Christ and His Word, it's as though you are making a deposit of spiritual capital. And every time you obey the Lord, He immediately matches your spiritual contribution of obedience. One day you'll look around and begin to see that your children are picking up momentum spiritually that they will pass on to their children. And it's quite probable that your compound interest will begin to pick up steam right about the time you reach the end of your earthly life. Just as you are ready to check out, the compounding effect will begin to pick up momentum beyond your wildest dreams.

This is estate planning at its finest. And when you leave this kind of spiritual inheritance to your children, it's all tax-free.

Now you have to stay with me here. I am not talking about earning your way to heaven. That is impossible. And most of you understand this. But there may be someone reading this who doesn't understand it. So let me take a couple of paragraphs to explain this. It's critical that you understand. There are men who think they are Christian fathers who are *not* Christian fathers. And they are pretty good guys. They don't cheat on their wives and they don't cheat on their taxes. But they are making a fundamental mistake. They are embracing Christianity on their terms. You can't do that. If you are going to be a Christian, you have to come on God's terms.

A lot of people are trying to earn God's favor and forgiveness through doing good works. And there are hundreds of thousands of fathers who view Christianity this way. But they have completely missed it. God does not operate on those terms.

The only way that any of us ever reach eternal life is through grace. Sheer, unadulterated, grace—apart from any human work or merit. In other words, God gives you something you don't deserve. And the reason you don't deserve it is that you have sinned against God. And you know in your gut that you have sinned. Every person reading this has sinned. I've sinned and you have sinned. We've gotten ourselves in a hole we can never get out of. Only God can get us out. But we only get out *His* way.

Eternal life cannot be earned. It can only be given by God the Father through His Son, the Lord Jesus Christ. Are you still with me? The way that a person becomes a Christian is to throw himself on the mercy of God and to ask God's forgiveness of his sins. The reason that God will forgive your sins is that Jesus went to the cross and paid for your sins by His own blood.

> But God, being rich in mercy, because of His great love with which He loved us, even when we were dead in our transgressions, made us alive together with Christ (by grace you have been saved), and raised us up with Him, and seated us with Him in the heavenly places, in Christ Jesus, in order that in the ages to come He might show the surpassing riches of His grace in kindness toward us in Christ Jesus. For by grace you have been saved through faith; and that not of yourselves, it is the gift of God; not as a result of works, that no one should boast.
> (Eph. 2:4–9)

That pretty well sums it up, doesn't it? Forgiveness of sins is a result of God's grace and mercy.

Have you asked Christ to be the Lord and Savior of your life? Do you realize that you have no hope to know God and to be forgiven by Him other than turning your whole life over to Christ?

When you submit your life to Christ, He will begin to change you in a number of ways. And one of the most important changes will be that you won't be just a father. You will be a *Christian* father.

Let me bottom-line this one more time because eternity is hanging on your understanding of this. *The Christian father is not trying to earn his way to heaven.* Salvation has been sovereignly given to him. Eternal life and the forgiveness of sins are a free gift. A Christian father realizes the enormity of the gift that he has been given and, as a result, he begins a journey of living in obedience to the Word of God out of a deep sense of gratitude for what God has given to him. And this is where compound interest comes in.

When God sees a man who prefers righteousness to sin, and that preference for righteousness is lived out in his attitudes, his treatment of his wife and kids, and the way he handles himself on the job, then that is a man whom God will bless. But God will not just simply bless that man. God will bless his children.

Bamboo farmers know all about compound interest. As a matter of fact, they stake their entire existence on it.

Growing bamboo is tough. Especially growing the supreme grade of bamboo. In Malaysia, there is a strain of very valuable bamboo that takes great wisdom and patience to cultivate. Here's how you do it.

- In the first year, you plant the seed, water, and fertilize. Nothing visible happens.
- In the second year, you continue to carefully water and fertilize. Nothing visible happens in the second year either.
- In the third year, water and fertilizer are even more necessary, yet nothing happens. There is absolutely no visible

  indication that your three years of work are even close to
  being successful.

- The fourth year comes around and water and fertilizer must
  still be applied, in the right amounts and at the right time.
  But you guessed it. Nothing happens.

- In the fifth year you again diligently water and fertilize.
  And the bamboo grows ninety feet in thirty days.

Not nine inches in thirty days; not nine feet in thirty days;
ninety feet in thirty days. From zilch to the height of a nine-
story building in thirty days.

That's what you call compound interest (actually it's more
like a zero-coupon bond, but you get the point).

It's not too late for you to begin compounding interest
as a father. There's nothing more that God would enjoy doing
than opening an interest-bearing account for you that will
be in your family for generations. That's certainly what He
has done for my friend Crawford Loritts.

Crawford and I have been friends for nearly fifteen years.
Perhaps you've had the privilege of hearing Crawford speak
at Promise Keepers. Crawford is a gifted communicator who
walks the talk.

Every time I'm with Crawford, I think *compound interest.*
In Crawford's study, he has on his wall a family tree that was
handwritten by his grandfather Milton. It's quite a document.
It begins with a man by the name of Peter Loritts. Peter was
a slave who gained his freedom at the end of the Civil War.
Crawford tells his story in his book *Never Walk Away.*[5]

About 130 years ago, Crawford's great-grandfather Peter
helped establish a small town not far from what is now the
Charlotte Motor Speedway. Peter had worked very hard all
of his life, and had somehow managed to scrape together a
few hundred dollars. With that money, Peter was able to buy
some acreage. The land that Peter bought eventually became

the town of Conover, North Carolina. A number of former slaves and their families comprised the town of Conover. Peter donated some land so that they could build their own church and have their own cemetery.

Peter could neither read nor write. But Peter loved the Lord Jesus, and he knew the Bible from the sermons and stories that he had heard. Peter obeyed the Bible to the best of his ability because he loved the Savior of the Bible.

Peter found a godly woman and married her. They were privileged with three children, two sons and a daughter. One of the boys was named Milton, and he's the one who wrote out the family tree. Milton and his wife had seven boys and seven girls. And one of those boys, in fact, the youngest boy, was Crawford's father. Crawford's dad went home to be with the Lord in 1996 at the age of eighty-one.

Peter taught his children to love and follow Jesus Christ. He showed his sons what it was to be a man. They saw him work hard, love their mother, and love them. Peter not only led his family, but he was always quick to help another family who had a financial need. His children learned by his example. As time went by, Peter's sons grew up and worked hard, loved their wives, and loved their children. Why? Because God was at the center of their homes. Reminds me of Joe Israel back in Deuteronomy 6.

Then the next generation came along, and once again, Jesus Christ was at the center of their lives. The boys of that generation became godly men and the girls became godly women. And Crawford's dad was of that generation. Crawford's dad would tell Crawford that, as a young boy, he would watch his grandfather Peter sitting on his rocker on the porch, passing each day singing praises to the Lord and telling his grandchildren about the greatness of Jesus.

God is still accruing His compound interest on Crawford's family. In the Loritts family there is a strong tradition of male leadership. There is a strong tradition of husbands loving their wives and children. There is a strong tradition that husbands in the Loritts family do not walk out on their families. And there is a strong tradition of Jesus Christ being at the center of each day's responsibilities. My friend Crawford is the fourth generation from the old slave Peter. And every time Crawford looks at the family tree, and every time Crawford looks in the mirror, he sees compound interest.

God is already favoring the fifth generation with that compound interest accrued to old Peter's account. When you meet Crawford's children, you see the goodness of God to the fifth generation. One of Crawford's sons has just enrolled in seminary to prepare for a lifetime of service to the same Lord that saved his great-great-grandfather.

Do you see what has happened in Crawford's family? Nearly 150 years later, old Peter is still anchoring his family. How did that phrase in Deuteronomy go? ". . . that you and your son and your grandson might fear the LORD." In the Loritts family, it is now "that you and your son and your grandson and your great-grandson and your great-great-grandson . . ." That's how God has blessed Peter Loritts. God is still paying interest on the original capital of daily obedience that was invested by a former slave who was serious about the daily fathering of his family.

So how do you lead your family for the next one hundred years? You do it the same way that Peter Loritts did it. You do it by being a godly father today. And then you do it again tomorrow. Putting away spiritual capital is living in obedience to Christ doing today what most men are too preoccupied to do. That's what old Peter did in North Carolina. He did what he needed to do each day to be a disciple of Jesus. That's the job of a Christian father. Not to be wildly successful. Not to be well known. Just to be faithful. God sees His faithful men. And God rewards His faithful men.

Every family chain, in order to survive and raise godly children, must somewhere have a man who has a godly vision, not only for his own children, but for the children of the generations to come. The fact of the matter is this: One man with vision who is anchored in Christ can influence his family and the generations to come for hundreds of years. If there's no old Peter in your family chain, then God is calling you to become that anchor. If your family has been drifting, it's time for your family to get anchored. And if you're the father, then guess what? God wants you to be the anchor.

And there's something that you should know. When that father who was an anchor is in eternity, he will be surrounded by hundreds and even thousands of people whom he has never met. These thousands of people will hug him and kiss him and do everything they can to get next to him. Why? Because he was the anchor of their family chain.

Anchors by themselves are useless. In order to be of value and to keep the family from drifting, the anchor must find something to grasp. Every anchor man who has ever affected a family for generations has grabbed on to a Rock. The same Rock. The only Rock.

And as the old hymn says,

> *This rock is Jesus, yes, he's the one,*
> *This rock is Jesus, the Only One.*
> *Be very sure, be very sure,*
> *Your anchor holds, and grips the solid rock.*

Do you know what's wrong with Dennis Rodman and Howard Stern? Their family chains didn't have a Peter. They didn't have an anchor. And that's why they both are drifting. Dennis and Howard desperately need to have a head-on collision. Straight into the Rock.

Wise fathers have a strong grip on the Lord Jesus. But here's the good news. The Lord Jesus has an even stronger grip on you than you have on Him. You can never grip Him as tight as He can grip you. And if you are in His grip, He will guarantee that your anchor holds. And by His grace, it will hold for countless generations to come: "Therefore know that the LORD your God, He is God, the faithful God who keeps covenant and mercy for a thousand generations with those who love Him and keep His commandments" (Deut. 7:9 NKJV).

—2—

IT TAKES MORE THAN SPERM

"If we stay on the current course, one day the United States will be known as the country of the founding fathers . . . with no fathers to be found."

—Dr. Wade Horn

It was a full-page ad in *USA Today*. The page was divided from top to bottom into two columns.

On the left-hand side of the page it simply said: *What it takes to be a father.* Underneath was a blown-up, magnified picture of a single sperm. On the right-hand side of the page the heading read:

What it takes to be a dad.

- Read to your children.
- Keep your promises.
- Go for walks together.
- Let your children help with household projects.
- Spend time one-on-one with each child.

- Tell your children about your own childhood.
- Go to the zoo, museums, ball games as a family.
- Set a good example.
- Use good manners.
- Help your children with their homework.
- Show your children lots of warmth and affection.
- Set clear, consistent limits.
- Consider how your decisions will affect your children.
- Listen to your children.
- Know your children's friends.
- Take your children to work.
- Open a savings account for your children.
- Resolve conflict quickly.
- Take your children to a place of worship.
- Make a kite together.
- Fly a kite together.

You get the idea.

It takes a man to be a dad.

It was a great ad. And it cost a lot of money to run nation-wide. So why did the Ad Council and the National Fatherhood Initiative drop so many bucks to make a distinction between what it takes to be a father and what it takes to be a dad?

They did it because we are in a crisis. A fathering crisis.

I don't speak Chinese. But I have been told by those who do that in the Chinese language, the word for "crisis" is made up of just two characters. One means "danger." The other means "opportunity."

That pretty much sums up a "crisis."

A crisis is a time of obvious danger. And, usually, some-where away from the harsh glare of that danger is a concealed opportunity.

J. Allen Petersen has been encouraging Christian families for decades. He is a Christian counselor and writer and a hus-band and father. Petersen knows full well the meaning of the word *crisis*. I'll let him relate the story:

> Every nook and cranny of the big 747 was crowded. It took off in the middle of the night in Brazil where I'd been speak-ing. As it moved into the night I started to doze. I don't know how long I slept, but I was starting to wake when I heard a strong voice announcing "We have a very serious emergency." Three engines had gone out because of fuel contamination, and the other engine would go any sec-ond.
>
> The steward said in English, "Now you must do exactly as we tell you. Don't think of doing anything we do not suggest. Your life depends on us. We are trained for your safety, so you must do exactly as we tell you."
>
> Then he rattled this off in Portuguese. Everybody looked soberly at one another.
>
> The steward said, "Now pull down the curtains, in a few minutes we are going to turn off the lights."
>
> My thoughts exclaimed, "Lord."
>
> The plane veered and banked, as the crew tried to get it back to the airport. The steward ran up and down the aisle and barked out orders, "Now take that card out of the seat pocket and I want you to look at the diagram." You know, I've flown millions of miles over the world and here I thought I had the card memorized, but I panicked because I couldn't find the crazy card. Everybody looked stunned as we felt the plane plunge down.
>
> Finally the steward said, "Now tighten the seat belts as tight as you can, and pull up your legs and bury your head

in your lap." We couldn't look out to see where we were—high or low.

I peeked around—the Portuguese were crossing themselves, and I thought, "This is it. This is serious. I can't believe this. I didn't know this was going to happen tonight. I guess this is it." And I had a crazy sensation.

Then the steward's voice broke into my consciousness, barking out in machine-gun fashion, "Prepare for impact." At a time like that, involuntarily from deep inside of us, something comes out that's never structured, planned or rehearsed. And all I could do was pray. Everybody started to pray. I found myself praying in a way I never thought of doing. As I buried my head in my lap and pulled my knees up, as I was convinced it was over I said, "Oh, God, thank you. Thank you for the incredible privilege of knowing you. Life has been wonderful." And as the plane was going down my last thought, my last cry, "Oh, God, my wife! my children!"[1]

When everything in life that seems so important is suddenly about to be taken away, something called perspective begins to take center stage. And when a man is facing death squarely in the eye, it comes right down to the fact that on this earth, there is nothing more important to him than his wife and children.

Petersen's plane made it back to the airport. He walked back into the foreign terminal, a nervous wreck and struggling for perspective:

As I wandered about in the middle of the night in the airport with a knot in my stomach and cotton in my mouth, I couldn't speak. I ached all over.

I thought, "What did I do? What did I say? What were my thoughts? Why did I think that?" I wondered, "What was the bottom line?"

Here's the bottom line: relationships.[2]

Not every father in America reaches the same conclusion that Petersen did. Some fathers come to the conclusion that there is something more important than their wives and children. It's not unusual for a man to walk out on his family and think that he can still be a father. But kids who are abandoned by their fathers know the truth. Their lives have been altered. The family has died. And things will never be the same. They intuitively understand the truth. It takes more than sperm to be a father. It takes commitment.

But commitment can be hard. Commitment can cost you something. And a lot of fathers simply aren't willing to pay the price. This is why we are in a crisis. And this fathering crisis is huge.

I'm not trying to hype you or be overly dramatic. I'm telling you the truth.

So what's the point of this chapter? I'm writing this chapter to persuade you never ever to leave your wife and your children. *There can be no fathering without commitment.* To be a father you must first be committed to your marriage. Committed to your kids. Committed to staying instead of leaving.

A real dad does more than simply produce children. A real dad keeps his promises. He chooses to work through the tough times, for the sake of his children. He refuses to abdicate being the head of his home. He leads his family and loves them. He provides for them and protects them, both emotionally and physically. These things he cannot do once he walks out the door. Some fathers are no longer with their children because they were forced to leave by a spouse who filed for divorce. They didn't choose to leave, they were forced to leave. They are in a completely different category from the fathers who decide to walk out.

A father who walks away from his family has walked away from fathering. And when he walks away from fathering, he has withdrawn the very thing his children need to grow up to be healthy adults. This is the simple, biblical truth that our culture wishes to deny, but that countless studies are beginning to overwhelmingly support.

A BANQUET OF CONSEQUENCES

David Blankenhorn has written a gritty book titled *Father-less America*. And in it he makes the picture very clear:

> The United States is becoming an increasingly fatherless society. A generation ago, an American child could reasonably expect to grow up with his or her father.
>
> Today, an American child can reasonably expect not to. . . . This astonishing fact is reflected in many statistics, but here are the two most important. Tonight, about 40 percent of American children will go to sleep in homes in which their fathers do not live. Before they reach the age of eighteen, more than half of our nation's children are likely to spend at least a significant portion of their childhoods living apart from their fathers. Never before in this country have so many children been voluntarily abandoned by their fathers.[3]

Such abandonment has consequences. And the consequences of one man's abandonment spread like ripples through a still pond, affecting us all.

It was Robert Louis Stevenson who said, "Everybody, sooner or later, sits down to a banquet of consequences." Let me introduce you briefly to the consequences banquet that has been set before us by an increasingly fatherless America:

- 85 percent of all children who exhibit behavioral disorders come from fatherless homes.

- 90 percent of all homeless and runaway children are from fatherless homes.
- 71 percent of all high school dropouts come from fatherless homes.
- 75 percent of all adolescent patients in chemical abuse centers come from fatherless homes.
- 63 percent of youth suicides are from fatherless homes.
- 70 percent of juveniles in state-operated institutions come from fatherless homes.
- 85 percent of all youths sitting in prisons grew up in fatherless homes.
- 80 percent of rapists come from fatherless homes.

It's time for someone to get on the intercom and say, "We have a very serious emergency."

Stop and think about this for a minute. By the year 2000, we are going to be in a situation where almost half of the children in America will live in a fatherless home. Not one out of twenty, or one out of ten. One out of every two kids in this country will be raised without a father. There's something very wrong and frightening about that picture.

> We now know from a careful examination of the evidence that today's fatherlessness has led to social turmoil—damaged children, unhappy children, aimless children, children who strike back with pathological behavior and violence. . . . The repercussions go far beyond children to include a steady deterioration in the lives of adult men and women. If present trends continue, our society could be on the verge of committing social suicide.[4]

Fathers count. Fathers who stay, that is. It takes more than sperm to make a difference in a child's life.

In 1980, Dr. James Dobson made an uncanny observation:

The western world stands at a great crossroads in its history.

It is my opinion that our very survival as a people will depend upon the presence or absence of male leadership in millions of homes. . . . I believe, with everything within me, that husbands hold the keys to preservation of the family.[5]

In the seventeen years since Dobson penned those words, male absence has skyrocketed. And he was right. We are *not* surviving. Why do Blankenhorn and others suggest that we are well on our way to social suicide? Because male absence adds up to no male leadership in millions of homes. That's how a nation commits social suicide. And we don't even need Kevorkian to help us.

We are killing ourselves, and we are doing it with two lethal injections. The first is the bearing and rearing of children "out of wedlock," or illegitimacy. It should come as no surprise that illegitimacy is growing at astronomical proportions, or that illegitimacy produces more illegitimacy. How can a young man fill a responsibility that no man has ever filled in his life?

But until now, illegitimacy has been mostly an inner-city problem. It is, however, quickly becoming a problem for the rest of America. Most of us know someone who has been touched by the heartbreak of illegitimacy.

But most of the men reading this book are not fathering illegitimate children, nor is it in their immediate plans. The vast majority are married with kids. That's why you've picked up this book on fathering. The primary threat to you and your family is not illegitimacy. It is divorce.

Divorce is the second lethal killer of fatherhood. And it is killing fathers just like you and me. That's why we need to deal with it head-on.

Divorce is not a comfortable subject. Talking about divorce is like having a conversation with a guy who is not socially well adjusted. When he talks to you, he gets about four inches from your face. And stays there. That's a very uncomfortable situation. Some of you are divorced and some of you come from divorced homes. It's a painful subject because so many have been affected by divorce. That is one of the reasons that we don't like to talk about it, but that's also the reason we must talk about it. Divorce is devastating to fathers and mothers and children. And it's just too common and prevalent to ignore.

You are reading this book because you are interested in being a better father. You already know that it takes more than sperm to be a father. And here we are smack in the middle of talking about divorce. Why am I talking about divorce when you want to talk about fathering? Because divorce is the number one way the enemy destroys fathers.

SATAN'S HIT LIST

There is something you need to know. If you are a father, Satan is out to get your hide. Fathers are the key and he knows that. The battle he is waging for your heart is an all-out, aggressive, and vicious one. He has no scruples and he will stop at nothing. And whether you believe that or not doesn't really matter to him. His goal is to derail you and render you useless as a father. In fact, Satan really doesn't mind if you read a book on biblical fathering. As long as you don't become too committed to your wife. That's why he will try to keep you from finishing this chapter.

There are three groups of fathers that Satan wants to derail from finishing this chapter.

1. There are the guys who have divorced their families, but know it was wrong and want to turn their lives around. If

you are divorced, you probably would rather not think about the past failures and mistakes of your life. But let me ask you to do something. Hang in there for a few more pages. Don't let Satan neutralize and derail you. My guess is that you still want to reach out to your children and reduce the gulf that has been created by divorce. But you will never be able to reach them without God's wisdom on marriage and divorce.

There is one other thing. You may have remarried (or one day will), and you want this marriage to last. This time you want to do things right. As I speak to men around the country, I find that some of the most highly motivated men I meet are those who have been through the tragedy of divorce. These men never want to go through divorce again. So they are determined to make a change in their lives. If you are one of those men, then you also need God's wisdom. One mistake doesn't need to lead to another. You *can* do things right from this point forward.

2. The second group Satan would like to derail is the men who haven't left their wives and children . . . yet. But some of them, in their hearts, are starting to entertain the idea that it might be "better" if they leave. They are still going to church and doing a lot of the right things. But underneath the surface, all is not well. If you are privately thinking about leaving, I must tell you something up front. My goal is to stop you dead in your tracks. You may not realize it, but you are walking into a trap. Divorce never delivers what it promises; divorce only kills. It kills families and wives and children and, yes, eventually it kills fathers. God wants you and your children to have life, and have it abundantly. He wants you to know the truth about divorce.

3. The last group is the vast majority of fathers who are reading this book. You are the ones who never intend to divorce. You are committed. You are thinking right now, *I would never leave my wife and kids.* But I've talked to too

many guys who have said they'd never do it, who *have* done it. I'm talking about Christian guys. Christian guys who had it all together.

Seven years ago I wrote a book to men that was titled *Point Man*. It was a book about being the spiritual leader of your family and being a one-woman kind of man. Several months after *Point Man* came out, I got a call from a pastor. He told me that in his message the previous Sunday he had held up a copy of *Point Man* in each of their three services and said, "This book is required reading for every man in this church. And beginning in two weeks, I am going to personally lead a study of this book for our men on Sunday nights." He ordered five hundred copies, and said that they may eventually need a thousand.

He took over seven hundred men from his congregation through the study. He was equipping his men to be the spiritual leaders their wives and children wanted them to be.

Six months later, he left his wife and children.

If Satan could get to him, he could get to me. And he could get to you. Your armor may be thick, but he knows your point of weakness. He knows where the seams and holes are, and he will not hesitate, at the right moment, to thrust the sword of death. Do you want your marriage and family to survive and thrive? Do you want to anchor your family for the next hundred years? Then keep reading. Don't let Satan derail you.

BASKETBALL IN BAKERSFIELD

It's 1956. I'm seven years old and I'm in second grade in Bakersfield, California. I'm across the street at Craig's house. As we're playing basketball in his driveway, I say, "Hey, Craig, where's your dad? I never see your dad around."

Craig replies, "My dad doesn't live here. My mom and dad are divorced."

And I say, "What's that?"

Can you imagine that a kid could be in second grade and not know what divorce is? I was astonished when Craig told me about divorce. I didn't know that divorce existed. I had never heard of divorce. You see, as a seven-year-old kid in 1956, I didn't know anyone who had been divorced. No one in my family had been divorced, none of our friends at church had been divorced, and out of about twenty kids in our class at school, Craig was the only one from a divorced home. In 1956, the vast majority of men knew that it took more than sperm to be a father. It took a willingness to stay in a marriage and be a father on a daily basis.

Today, just forty years later, things have completely reversed. In one generation, we have gone from a culture of marriage to a culture of divorce. I guarantee you that there is not a second grader in America who is not familiar with the word *divorce*. Now, in many second-grade classrooms across our nation, if a child is still living with his original parents, he is in the minority.

Back in 1956, who would have believed that the institution of marriage was in serious danger? If someone had told us that we were about to enter a crisis, and that the crisis would be a national marriage crisis, none of us would have believed it.

Parents didn't divorce in 1956. But by 1966 society was changing its mind. In 1969, California introduced the first "no-fault" divorce law and in the next five years, forty-five other states joined them. By 1985, all fifty states had established no-fault divorce.[6]

In 1956, about 300,000 children across America watched their parents divorce. In 1996, nearly twenty-three *million* children did not live with their biological fathers.[7] This shift is nothing less than astonishing: "The scale of marital break-down in the West since 1960 has no historical precedent that I know of, and seems unique. There has been nothing like it for the last 2000 years."[8]

We need to make sure that this scale is in perspective. Not everyone who is divorced wanted the divorce. I know men who are divorced who did everything within their power to make the marriage work. Their wives took advantage of the no-fault divorce law and went ahead and split the family. I know women who are divorced who had the same situation. They were willing to do anything to make the marriage work, but their husbands went ahead and severed the family. It is a tragedy when the laws of a nation not only give permission for, but *promote,* the self-centered motives of an irresponsible mate. The fact is that no-fault divorce destroys a lot of innocent people.

YOUR-FAULT DIVORCE

No-fault divorce says that a marriage can be destroyed at the whim of one partner. And it's nobody's fault. If our country ran business this way, we would be living in economic chaos and collapse. But here's the naked truth about no-fault divorce. No-fault divorce is always someone's fault. And if you're the one who walks, then it is your fault.

If, on the other hand, you were willing to work on the relationship, but your spouse wasn't, then it wasn't your fault. You're not perfect, but you didn't desert your post. God will honor you for your commitment.

No-fault divorce has led to a marriage crisis. And right on its heels has followed the fathering crisis. It's impossible to separate the marriage crisis from the fathering crisis. They are as inseparable as identical twins. Just as one twin comes first and then shortly thereafter comes the other, so the marriage crisis showed up first, and then on its heels came the fathering crisis.

No-fault divorce has also "lowered the standard." A few years ago, Promise Keepers adopted the theme "Raise the Standard" for their national stadium events. That's a great concept in a culture that is continually lowering the standard. Lowering the standard has become our way of simply eliminating the problem.

If the drug problem is getting out of control, what do we do? We legalize drugs! We lower the standard!

If illegitimacy grows out of control, what do we do? We legitimize it. We say that, contrary to the old television series, *father really doesn't know best.* Fatherhood as we have known it really *isn't* important! The presence of a father in the home really *isn't* necessary any longer for the well-being of the child! This is precisely what voices in our nation are saying. And these people are serious.

> One hundred, fifty, or even thirty years ago the premise that a child should live with a father in a nuclear family was universally held. Father absence was considered a tragedy, and a father who left his children was considered unmistakably deviant. Not so today. Divorce when children are involved is well-accepted by more than three quarters of the (American) population. And there is a growing acceptance of childbirth without a father in the home, especially among the young.[9]

Once again, somebody is trying to lower the standard. But lowering the standard never solves a problem. It only creates other problems.

God has never called His men to lower the standard. We are to raise the standard. And how do we raise the standard? *We listen to the One who sets the standard.* God hasn't just raised the standard. He has *set* the standard from before the beginning of time. Listen to what He says about divorce: "'I hate divorce,' says the LORD, the God of Israel" (Mal. 2:16).

Note that God doesn't lower the standard. Note that He doesn't mince words. Note that He's not running for office and reading polls. He just puts it right on the table.

God hates divorce. And you should hate it too. When you hate divorce, you don't consider it an option. Divorce is an enemy. When you hate divorce, you don't sign prenuptial agreements before you get married. When you hate divorce, you don't leave a marriage just because you are not happy.

Why does God hate divorce? Let me offer several reasons:

- God hates divorce because it breaks something up that He doesn't want broken up: the family.
- God hates divorce because it devastates women when their husbands abandon them for other women, and vice versa.
- God hates divorce because it kills kids. It crushes kids. It extinguishes the life in their little emotional hearts. God hates divorce because He loves children. Children need fathers.
- God hates divorce because it sets in motion a destructive pattern for future generations. Adult children from divorced homes divorce at a rate *four times greater* than kids from homes where there was no divorce. When divorce enters into a family chain, it tends to stay there—unless Jesus Christ intervenes.

CLEAVE, DON'T LEAVE

Do you want to raise the standard? Then there is something very specific that you can do. If you are married, here's your assignment. And you may want to write this down. Are you ready?

Ward Cleave. Say what?

Do you remember the TV show *Leave It to Beaver*? The star of the show was Theodore "Beaver" Cleaver. But the real star was his father, Ward Cleaver. Ward Cleaver was the kind of father that Hollywood used to portray as a role model. He was a churchgoing, hardworking, balanced, loving father who led his family. And there was something else about Ward Cleaver. He would never divorce his wife. It would never enter into his mind because it would violate his value system.

Although it was never stated in the show, Ward Cleaver lived by the truth of Genesis 2:24: "For this cause a man shall leave his father and his mother, and shall *cleave* to his wife; and they shall become one flesh" (emphasis added).

The word *cleave* means to "cling" or "adhere to." That describes Ward Cleaver. When it came to his wife he wasn't going to walk. He had "adhered to" June Cleaver and he was going to stay put for the rest of his life. Divorce was not an option for Ward Cleaver. That's why I call him Ward Cleave.

The Ward Cleave, Genesis 2:24 prescription is this: *Never, ever, ever, leave your wife*. Did you get that? That's your job. You stay married. You don't walk. You don't lower the standard. You raise it. No matter how tough it gets, you stay with it.

After all, isn't that what you promised to do? You committed yourself for life. No one made you do it. You weren't threatened or drugged when you said it. You said it of your own volition. You said that you would be committed

- in sickness and in health,
- for richer or poorer,
- for better or worse.

So your wife has lost her health? Maybe she's lost a breast to cancer. Or maybe she has plummeted into a deep depression. Then it's time to step up to the plate and be a man.

That business you started didn't get off the ground? You've had to declare bankruptcy? That shouldn't affect your commitment to your wife one iota. Sure things are hard financially, and that's difficult for anyone to go through. But what in the world does that have to do with leaving?

Things aren't going well at home? It seems that you and your wife don't see eye to eye on anything? There's no communication and there's no romance in the marriage? In other words, when you look at your marriage, it's not better, it's worse? Well, that's exactly why you made the commitment. And there's no rational, biblical reason to walk. There is a selfish reason to walk. But let me warn you. If you ever do it, you'll just start another crisis.

Perhaps now you've got a marriage crisis. But if you leave, you're going to have a fathering crisis. Trust me. That's something that you don't want to do. That's jumping from the frying pan into the fire.

Legally, you have been given the right to walk away from your wife and children. There's nothing legally to hold you to that marriage. But there is something morally and spiritually to hold you and it's Genesis 2:24. God expects you to Ward Cleave.

You are one flesh with your wife. There are times in every marriage when we don't feel that we are one. But we are. And God wants the two who are one to remain one. Let me tell you who else wants the two who have become one to remain one. Your kids do.

Maybe you saw the movie *Mrs. Doubtfire*. It's a story about a dad whose wife divorces him and he's trying to get back with his kids. So he comes up with the idea of dressing as an older woman and applying for the job of nanny for his children. When you really step back and analyze *Mrs. Doubtfire*, it's a Hollywood attempt to put a positive spin on the real-life devastation of divorce for children.

In the closing scene of the film, Mrs. Doubtfire offers some grandmotherly advice to a little girl who is trying to understand why her parents have broken up. "Some parents, when they're angry, they get along much better when they don't live together," says Mrs. Doubtfire. "They don't fight all the time and they can become better people and much better mommies and daddies."[10]

When I first heard those words in the movie, I was reminded of Winston Churchill's description of Lawrence of Arabia: "He was not in complete harmony with the normal."

Neither is Mrs. Doubtfire. The way to become a better person is *not to* divorce. The way to become a better person is to get over your own selfishness and personal need for immediate self-gratification and stay with the marriage and do everything you have to do to resolve your conflict. God wants you to stay. Your kids want you to stay. So don't leave. The worst possible thing you can do is to sever that marriage relationship. All you will do by trying to escape one crisis is to create another. And you really don't want to do that.

Do you want your kids to be statistics in the fathering crisis? Of course you don't. Then don't ever leave. And don't ever think about leaving. It's not an option. It doesn't exist. You're a better man than that.

If you are a Christian, you have been given the Holy Spirit. He lives within you. And He is the One who will enable you to keep your commitment. You are not alone; He is with you. He knows your frustration, He knows your disappointment, He knows your failures. Call out to Christ and ask for His help, and He will give you the power to do the right thing.

LEADING IN LOVE

God is in the business of turning around tough situations. It may not happen overnight. But then again, it doesn't need to happen overnight. You're not going anywhere. You're staying. You're committed. And because you're committed, God can take you through a process that will make you a mature, wise man.

You need not wait around for a miracle to happen, or for your wife to make a change. You take the first step. You take the lead. God has told you where to begin:

- Start by loving her as Christ loves His church (Eph. 5:25).
- Start by living with her in an understanding way (1 Peter 3:7).
- Start by granting honor to her as a fellow heir of the grace of life (1 Peter 3:7).

You may be saying, "This is some place to start! God doesn't ask much, does He?" But it is the only place to start. Love her, understand her, honor her. Make her the top priority of your life. She may not respond. She may leave. But don't you leave.

When a guy lays aside his own agenda, humbles himself, confesses his sin, and starts to listen to the Holy Spirit, he has also incurred the blessing of God upon his life. God honors the man who honors his wife and children.

THE HEARTS OF THE FATHERS

Malachi 4:6 has something to say to the father who has already left. And it has something to say to every father who has stayed.

Malachi 4:6 is the last verse in Malachi. And this is significant. It is significant because Malachi is the last book of the Old Testament. And Malachi 4 is the last chapter of the last book in the Old Testament. And verse 6 of Malachi 4 is the last verse in the last chapter of the last book in the Old Testament.

Here's the interesting thing. Between the end of Malachi and the beginning of the New Testament there was a four-hundred-year gap. And in those four hundred years, God was silent. He gave no revelation.

Did you catch that? God didn't speak again for four hundred years. Not four years, or fourteen. But four hundred years.

Let me ask you a question. If you were God, and you weren't going to speak for four hundred years, what would be the last thing that you would say? What would you want your people to remember for four hundred years?

Here's what God said: "And he will turn the hearts of the fathers to the children, and the hearts of the children to their fathers, lest I come and strike the earth with a curse" (NKJV).

God finishes the Old Testament by talking about fathers and their kids! Israel was in the midst of its own fathering crisis. And the answer to Israel's problems lay at the feet of dads. God's blessing was contingent upon the repentant hearts of fathers, turned back toward their children. This is what God wanted to leave indelibly printed upon their minds for the next four hundred years.

Are you surprised that Israel had a fathering crisis too? It shouldn't surprise us when we read the whole book of Malachi. Israel's fathering crisis also began with a marriage crisis: "Because the LORD has been a witness between you and the wife of your youth, against whom you have dealt treacherously, though she is your companion and your wife by covenant" (Mal. 2:14).

Did not the Lord make the husband and wife one? Why? That you might bring forth a godly family. Take heed then, to your spirit, and *let no one deal treacherously against the wife of your youth*.

The men of Israel were walking away from their wives. And it had led to a full-blown fathering crisis. Human nature never changes, does it? It is the same now as it was over two thousand years ago. And so is God.

God sees fatherless America and He knows how to fix it. God saw fatherless Israel, and He told them how to fix it. "Love the wife of your youth," He said, "and turn your hearts back toward your children."

Four hundred years later, God finally spoke again. Through the writer of the gospel of Luke, we read about a rugged prophet named John the Baptist. John the Baptist was the first prophet from God since Malachi, four hundred years before. And John the Baptist declared the arrival of Jesus, the Messiah. It was said of John, that he "[turned] the hearts of the fathers back to the children" (Luke 1:17). And under John's ministry, a revival began in Israel.

Just as in the days of Malachi and the days of John the Baptist, revival and the blessing of God are closely linked to a father's heart. Fathers are key to the survival of their families *and* their nation.

And, just as in the days of Malachi and John the Baptist, God is still ready to act. He is our only hope. Apart from Him there is no help for us as fathers. There is no solution to the marriage and fathering crises.

Wherever you are, God is ready to act on your behalf. No matter how great the pain of your marriage, He is there. If you are thinking about divorce, He is there. If you are already divorced, He is there. If the divorce was your fault, guess what. He's still there. If your life is nothing but a conglomeration of broken pieces, He is there. And if you reach out to

Him, no matter what mistakes you've made, there is hope. That's the truth, my friend.

From this day on, give your life completely to Him. If you haven't already, ask Him to take away your sin and give you eternal life. Ask Him to call the shots in your life. Ask Him to show you what to do. And then do it. He has a way of taking broken men and broken relationships and fixing them. I can't tell you how He will do it. I just know that's what He does. He's your Father. And if you'll listen up, He'll not only make you a better father . . . He will forge you into an anchor.

—3—

PLYMOUTH ROCK COACHING CLINIC

"It is a wise father that knows his own child."

—Shakespeare

George S. Patton was a legend in his own lifetime. That can only be legitimately said of a small number of men. But it was true of Patton. One of his fellow officers said at his memorial service, "We shall never look upon his like again."[1]

From an early age, Patton was groomed by his father for admission to the Virginia Military Institute. "When he graduated, he was second in his class and rated first in tactics, mathematics, Latin, geology and chemistry."[2] He was described by one who knew him well as "arrogant, a smart dresser, and he displayed classic chivalry toward ladies, making him a dashing, romantic figure."[3] "Devoutly religious (at least by his own standards), Patton also encouraged his men to attend chapel and rarely missed an opportunity to pray on his knees before his God."[4] According to one of his biographers, "Patton was a visionary who saw war clouds on the horizon and was determined to prepare for action."[5]

He was virtually fearless in combat. On one occasion, an enemy's bullet did find its way to him, but a ten-dollar gold piece in his pocket successfully deflected the bullet, leaving him with only a slight wound.[6]

Perhaps none of this information is new to you. Maybe you have read a biography about Patton or saw the movie that was released in 1970. But there's one problem. The George S. Patton I have just described is not the Patton of World War II. The Patton I have just described was the *grandfather* of the Patton whom America knows so well. He is the George S. Patton who died in 1864 from wounds sustained in the Civil War.

The George S. Patton that America is so familiar with was George S. Patton III. But the Patton of whom it was said, "We shall never look upon his like again" was his grandfather. The truth is that we did see his like again. And we saw it in his grandson. Let me tell you why we saw it again. There was a very strong tradition of good coaching in the Patton line. In Patton's family, the father was expected to coach his son so that he would be capable of effectively coaching his son. It had been that way for generations in the Patton family chain. The present link coached the future link.

Why is George S. Patton III such a great American hero, more than fifty years after his death in Germany? A strong case could be made that George S. Patton III was such a great leader because he grew up in a home where male leadership was modeled before his eyes. And the leadership of George S. Patton I was carried down to George S. Patton III by the example and leadership of George S. Patton II.

The leadership of one great military leader was strong enough to create another great leader two generations later. And the only reason that the Patton in between the two war heroes was not a war hero himself was that there was no war for him to show his stuff in. But he, too, was a leader of men and a tremendous father.

Everywhere Patton III looked he was surrounded by male leadership. He was raised on a ranch in southern California that was established by his grandfather. And this ranch was no ordinary ranch. The ranch where Patton was raised is now known as Orange County, California. Not the city of Orange, the *county* of Orange. It was George Patton's maternal grandfather who bought that land from the Spanish and then married into the family that owned Rancho Santa Ana. As the years went by, he planted hundreds of thousands of orange trees across the rich soil of his sprawling ranch. His landholdings included what is today the campus of UCLA, the city of Pasadena, the city of Riverside, and of course, most of Orange County. That's a lot of territory for one man to oversee and manage. But Patton's maternal grandfather, Benjamin Davis Wilson, was a visionary male leader. The George Patton of World War II was very fortunate. He received good coaching from both sides of his family.

Strong, balanced male leaders produce strong, balanced male leaders. That's why the George Patton of World War II was who he was. But not every man has the benefit of that kind of male coaching.

THE CONFUSED FATHER

I run into fathers all the time who are confused about their leadership responsibilities. And the reason they are confused about their fathering responsibilities is that they were not well coached by their fathers when they were growing up. A very successful businessman, who was also a very frustrated father, described his dilemma to his pastor:

You tell me that I'm supposed to be the head of my home. You challenge me to be a leader. I want to be the kind of man you are describing, but every time I try, I seem to fail. Is it because I don't understand what being a leader is all about? I guess my father was not much of a leader; perhaps I never had a chance to learn what was expected of me. What is an effective family leader anyway?[7]

Did you catch his closing question? This man is asking what an effective family leader is, because he grew up without one. Men who grow up with effective and balanced fathers do not ask what an effective family leader looks like. They have seen one in action. And intuitively they know how to coach when it is their time and place to do so.

I am convinced that most men in this nation have grown up with a real void deep inside of them. And it all relates to their relationship with their dad. If your father was a good family coach, then he taught you and motivated you. But if he wasn't, then it's inevitable that you are going to struggle with what it really means to be a father. Someone once said, "It is easier to build a boy than to mend a man."

Every man is indelibly marked by his relationship with his dad.

- When you think back to your relationship with your dad, do you experience any heartache?
- When you think back to your relationship with your dad, do you have a sense that he neglected you?
- When you think back to your relationship with your dad, do you feel any deep regret?
- When you think back to your relationship with your dad, is there a major disappointment?
- When you think back to your relationship with your dad, do you find yourself still trying to earn his approval and acceptance?

If you do, you certainly are not alone. Dr. George Vaillant has spent years studying the relationships between fathers and their grown sons. He has tracked numerous businessmen, professors, and scientists from their days in college through their forties and fifties. One of the most remarkable findings of his study with these men was that when Dr. Vaillant asked them, when they were forty-seven, about the most influential men in their lives, "in more than ninety-five percent of the cases, fathers were either cited as negative examples or were mentioned as people who were not influences."[8]

That is a staggering statistic. Dr. Vaillant interviews scores of successful men throughout America, and only 5 percent of those men cited their fathers as positive role models.

It has not always been that way. But that's exactly where we are. And that's why if you are reading these pages and are able to look back upon the influence of your father as warm, loving, and nurturing then you are in the minority. Because the majority of guys reading this book didn't experience a father like that.

How does a man who didn't have a positive fathering role model learn to be a good father? You show up for a coaching clinic. And you don't need to take two weeks off from work. You just need a couple of days to speed-model. At least, that's how Bear Bryant used to do it.

SPEED-MODELING

So how do you "speed-model"?[9] The concept is pretty simple. If someone in your particular field is doing something that is innovative, creative, effective, and successful, and you think that you could benefit from what he has learned, then you speed-model. You get on a plane and go hang out with him for twenty-four to forty-eight hours. You watch, you ask questions, and you listen. And then you go home and adapt what you learned from the model to fit your particular situation.

That's what Bear Bryant did at Alabama for many years. Bryant was one of the greatest coaches in the history of college football. And one reason that he was so successful in the nearly forty years that he coached was that he never became cocky or set in his ways. Bryant was always willing to learn and innovate. He was never too proud to learn from someone else. In fact, he was eager to learn.

Over those forty years, college football changed. Offensive systems evolved from the single wing, to the T-formation, to the wishbone, to the option. You throw in the shotgun and the pro set and you've got some very complex offensive schemes. And Bear Bryant flexed and learned every one of them.

One particular year Alabama was beat by a couple of teams using this new "wishbone." Bear Bryant considered any season with two losses not to be a good season. Alabama hadn't run the wishbone offense, but the next time Bama played those schools they beat both of them. And they did it using the wishbone. How did Bear Bryant change his entire offensive scheme in one off-season?

He called up Darrell Royal at the University of Texas and asked if he could come and visit him for a few days. Bear Bryant showed up in Austin with a couple of his assistant coaches, and for the next two days, Darrell Royal and his coaches showed them all the ins and outs of the wishbone.

The first time Bear Bryant heard about the wishbone he thought it was part of a chicken dinner. But before long, he had mastered it so completely that he ended up winning a national championship with it. The secret to his success was that he speed-modeled that offense from Darrell Royal.

If you are feeling confused about your role as a father, you can relax. Good fathering can be learned in the same way that Bear Bryant learned new offenses. You simply have to see it in action.

That's why I have written this book. In the rest of this book, we are going to speed-model fathering. So let's get on a mental plane and head to Austin. Actually, we're not going to Austin, because we're not trying to speed-model the wishbone. We want to speed-model biblical fathering. We're going to the Plymouth Rock Coaching Clinic.

Plymouth Rock? You mean the Plymouth Rock where the Pilgrims landed? You got it.

In the last five to ten years, numerous studies have been done on fathering in the United States. And what has become very clear is that the most noble time of fathering that our nation has ever seen was at the very beginning.

Why is it that in the 1990s so many men are unsure of what it means to be a father? Why is it that in the 1990s so many men have a father hunger that has never been satisfied in their relationships with their own fathers? The answer is that for nearly two hundred years we have been systematically dismantling the role and responsibilities of fathers in America. It's worth studying a little bit of history to understand how badly we have slipped and what we can do to get ourselves back in line with fathering the way that God intended for it to be.

Speed-Modeling the Master Fathers

When you think of Plymouth Rock you think of the Pilgrims. But the Pilgrims were part of a larger group of people called the Puritans. The Puritans were master fathers who produced master families. And the reason that they had such wonderful families is that they were people of the Bible.

- If you want to improve your golf game then spend a day or two with Jack Nicklaus.

- If you want to learn from the best model of fathering that this nation has ever seen, then check out the Puritans. These guys may have dressed weird, but they sure knew how to father.

The Puritans were godly people who left England to get a start in a new land. The Bible was central to their faith and their faith was lived out in their families. This is why they are so often referred to in negative terms. We often hear of an idea or a book being put down because it is "puritanical." Today, if a man is referred to as "puritanical," he is considered to be cold, narrow, unkind, and unfeeling . . . all the things you would never want in a father. But the truth is that to be called "puritanical" is actually a great compliment. What it really means is that you have a standard that is biblical and honoring to God. And a man who honors God in his fathering is anything but negative. He is balanced and effective. In other words, he is both affirming and firm. He is both strong and tender. You and I have been misled when it comes to our Puritan forefathers.

No one can ignore the strength of the Puritan families. And that strength can be traced to the centrality of the Christian father in the home.

THE SECRET OF THE PURITAN FATHERS

How are you feeling right now? Are you tired? Are you ready for a nap? Then don't read this next section right now. Go take a nap and come back to it when you've got a clear head and you can concentrate. Or drink a cup of coffee or a can of Jolt Cola. You need some juice to get into this next section.

The reason it's so important is that it contains some of the secrets that made the Puritan men such great fathers. Read it slowly and thoughtfully. There will be a quiz later. Just kidding. I've put in italics the really critical stuff.

> Between 1620 and 1640 New England absorbed a "Great Migration" of 20,000 men, women and children . . . the overwhelming majority of these settlers were Puritans, who often came to the New World with their ministers as pre-formed congregations settling the towns in and around Plymouth and Boston.[10]

The Puritans quickly built their churches and worshiped in them on Sunday. But *for the other six days of the week, the primary place of religious reflection and prayer was the household. Within each home the father was to play the role of the minister, leading his family in Bible readings and doctrinal explanation.*"[11]

> The male head of the household was the towering figure and unquestioned ruler, and by today's standards, his authority was stern and rigid. . . . Puritan children were at all times to show honor and respect for their fathers. Such unquestioned patriarchy was strongly upheld by the Christianity of the day. *Nevertheless, the Puritan father/husband was expected to treat his dependents with respect and restraint, and male gentleness in social relations was admired.* . . .
>
> Fatherhood was remarkably strong among the Puritans. . . . It was a substantial part of the Puritan man's deeply felt sense of duty toward others. *All adult men were expected to become fathers, and there was a large father presence in the lives of their children.*[12]

There was *a particularly high level of devotion to their children among Puritan fathers, one that . . . has not been equaled on a large scale since.*

Because the home was an economic production unit in which both fathers and mothers participated, fathering was an extension, if not a part of, the routine activities of daily life. . . . Sons, especially, worked side by side with their fathers from their earliest years until their own marriages. Sons were often close replicas of their fathers, and generational continuity from father to son was relatively smooth. . . .

Most direct care of infants and young children was performed by women; *but in a childrearing regimen that stressed authority, . . . and morality, the father was considered the primary parent. . . .* Where schools existed, the teachers were always men. *Yet most of the formal teaching was done by fathers in the home, where the emphasis was on the teaching of moral and religious matters.*

Fatherhood may have reached its height among the Puritans, at least for the time span of recent centuries, as an all-powerful, self-consuming, fully engaging activity for men . . . *the Puritan man's sense of identity was inseparable from his family and community obligations.* Through his role as head of the household, a man expressed his value to his community and provided for his wife and children with their social identity.[13]

As one contemporary scholar recently wrote, "Since Puritan times it has all been downhill for fathering."[14]

Why did it all go downhill? How did all of that good generational coaching begin to break down? David Blankenhorn does a pretty good job of answering that question. And his central thought is that instead of fathers being the centers of the family, they are now on the outside looking in:

In colonial America, fathers were seen as primary and irreplaceable caregivers. According to both law and custom, fathers bore the ultimate responsibility for the care and well-being of their children, especially older children. Throughout the eighteenth century, for example, child-rearing manuals were generally addressed to fathers, not mothers. Until the early nineteenth century, in almost all cases of divorce, it was established practice to award the custody of children to fathers. Throughout this period, fathers, not mothers, were the chief correspondents with children who lived away from home.

More centrally, fathers largely guided the marital choices of their children and directly supervised the entry of children, especially sons, into the world outside the home. Most important, fathers assumed primary responsibility for what was seen as the most essential parental task: the religious and moral education of the young. As a result, societal praise or blame for a child's outcome was customarily bestowed not (as it is today) on the mother but on the father.[15]

It used to be in America that almost every father took his coaching responsibilities seriously. It was his job to teach his children. And it was his job to motivate his children. These men were coaching their children and coaching them well. But somewhere along the line, men started bailing out on the fathering responsibilities. So who took up the slack? The women did.

In the 1830s, following the industrialization of printing, there was a surge in guides directed toward women which reflected the new view of children. *Indeed, the belief arose that women were morally superior to men*—pure, upright, sensitive, and the true civilizing force in life. It was now women who were supposed to raise their children to be morally straight (and also to keep their men on the proper moral path in an increasingly complex society). . . . In time, women became the teachers of religion, even taking over the long-time male activity of leading the family in its daily prayers.[16]

It was during this time that Josiah Gilbert Holland, a popular writer, said, "The foundation of our national character is laid by the mothers of the nation."[17] For nearly two hundred years, since those Puritan fathers arrived at Plymouth Rock with their families, it was the men who were setting the character of the nation. But by 1830, fathers began to drop back ten yards and punt the character issue to their wives. And that's when the fathering crisis and the coaching crisis began to take root.

THE GREAT TWO-HUNDRED-YEAR FATHER DISCONNECTION

So what has happened to fathering since the Puritans (Pilgrims) landed at Plymouth Rock?

Let me put it to you this way. Fathers got disconnected.

Have you ever been on the phone and suddenly gotten disconnected?

Well, then you know what happened to bring on the fathering crisis of our day. Some two hundred years ago, fathers got disconnected. And one disconnection led to another.

- Fathers got disconnected *physically* when the Industrial Revolution hit our country and fathers left their homes to go to work. Up until the Industrial Revolution men had worked in and around their homes. But for the first time in history a man's work removed him from the home for ten to twelve hours a day. Fathers were no longer a visible presence as family leader and overseer. Sons no longer matured and trained under the guiding hands of their fathers.

- Fathers got disconnected *spiritually* when they fell for the lie that women should have the moral and spiritual responsibility of the home. God clearly expects His men to spiritually lead their families. Godly women want the same thing.

- Fathers got disconnected *emotionally* from their children when they didn't fill the emotional tanks of their sons and daughters. That's why so many men in America feel such a great sense of loss in their relationships with their fathers. Their dads never filled their emotional tanks when they were boys. So these guys are literally running on empty. And when you are running on empty emotionally you've got nothing to give to anyone else.

Why are so many men clueless when it comes to coaching their own children? Because their fathers before them did not know how to father. Every time one father got disconnected from his family, and didn't reconnect, each subsequent link in his family chain was affected. And when that happens in numerous families over two hundred years, you end up with a complete crisis of fathers who don't know how to father. There are some family chains that have been disconnected for almost two hundred years. Maybe that's your family. If it is, it's time for a man to reestablish communication. And you are that man.

It's very possible that your father did not connect with you because his father did not connect with him. And his father did not connect with him. Somebody in your family chain did not take care of his link. And the rest of the links have suffered for it. You have suffered for it. Your father has suffered for it. Perhaps his father suffered for it. It's time to put a stop to all the suffering. It's time to put a new link in the family chain. What a fortunate man you are to have that opportunity. After years of disconnects, you get to be the guy who reconnects. Welcome to the coaching ranks.

So how do you reconnect? You get back on the phone and try to reestablish communication.

Has work disconnected you from your children? If so, you need to seriously rethink some things about your work. Every man struggles between the demands of his career and the desire to father his children. But if you and I are going to connect with our kids, we have to be physically present with them. It is as simple as that. You can't father at the office or on a plane. Does this sound tough? The great work of fathering has never been easy. But when God calls a man to do something, He always provides a way for him to do it. That's why we are going to spend the next couple of chapters on this issue.

Have you been disconnected from your kids emotionally? Physical presence alone doesn't guarantee good fathering. If your children are running on empty, and many children from good homes are, then you need to reestablish communication.

So how do you go about reconnecting? On pages 23–24 I quoted a long list of activities that fathers can do with their children. Go back to that list and pick five activities that you can do with your kids in the next sixty days. That's how you can begin to reconnect. And then pick five more and do those over the following sixty-day period. You'll be surprised how quickly you reestablish the connection that you want to have to their lives.

GOOD COACHES, LOUSY COACHES

There are good coaches and there are lousy coaches. Any guy who has spent any time at all playing ball has usually experienced both. So what's the difference between a good coach and a lousy coach?

Good coaches teach; lousy coaches don't. Good coaches motivate; lousy coaches don't.

I was watching a peewee football practice not too long ago. It was the first practice of the season. And for many of those boys, it was the first practice of their lives.

After the usual calisthenics, the coach assigned each boy to play a position. On the very first play, the fullback missed the handoff from the quarterback because he ran in the direction opposite from where the quarterback was turning to give him the ball. The coach immediately started yelling at the boy, "You're supposed to hit the two hole! The two hole!"

The little guy looked at the coach in complete bewilderment and asked, "What's the two hole?"

This coach had made a critical error. His error was that he didn't teach. He *assumed* that these eleven-year-olds had spent the first decade of their lives watching game films with Bill Walsh or Tom Landry.

He was very angry at his fullback for missing the two hole. But it had never crossed his mind that before you run a play you first explain what a "hole" is. And then you explain the numbering system for each hole before you ever have these kids take a snap from center. Good coaches assume nothing. And good coaches take the time to teach. So do good fathers.

The Puritans were great coaches. They knew how to teach. And they knew how to motivate. It's tough to play the game without a good coach.

It's tough to be a good father if you didn't have a good father. Your ability to father is greatly affected by how you were fathered. If biblical fatherhood was modeled for you, you've got a tremendous head start. But if it wasn't, you can still catch up. You really can.

One of the best coaches I ever had was Coach Coburn. He coached football and basketball, and he was also a shop teacher.

In his mid-thirties, Coach Coburn was tall and in pretty good shape. He obviously had played some ball in his day, although I don't recall that he ever mentioned it. But Coach Coburn never assumed that we automatically knew the game. He made sure that we all understood the plays. He made sure that we understood our positions. He took the time to teach us.

Coach Coburn was one of those coaches who command respect. He didn't ask for respect; it was just the only response that a twelve-year-old could have for a man like that.

Coach Coburn was firm but fair. He respected those twelve-year-old boys who were under his leadership. Come to think of it, that's probably why we had such great respect for him. I thoroughly enjoyed playing football and basketball for Coach Coburn. But halfway through basketball season, my family moved to a town four hundred miles away. And that's when I ran into Coach Sanders.

Coach Sanders was everything that Coach Coburn wasn't. He never really took the time to teach us. And he certainly never thought about how he could best motivate us. None of the guys respected him. Maybe that's because he didn't respect us. His favorite name for us was "you animals." When someone would fail to run the right play or would make a mental error, Coach Sanders would yell out, "You animal!" Come to think of it, the only thing that Coach Sanders was really good at was yelling. Back in the fifties, Walt Disney came out with a great movie about a faithful dog called *Old Yeller*. When I first heard about *Old Yeller,* I thought it was about Coach Sanders.

Coach Coburn taught his players; Coach Sanders didn't. Coach Coburn motivated his players; Coach Sanders didn't.

Both men were called "coach." But only one of them actually coached. The other just drew a paycheck.

Why was Coach Coburn such a great coach? Why did every twelve-year-old guy in our school want to be like him? Maybe it's because of the impact that Coach Coburn's father had on him.

You see, Coach Coburn's father was head of all the schools in our county. He went into administration after twenty years of teaching and coaching. He was respected as a man of character and integrity.

No wonder his son was such an excellent coach. Coach Coburn was a great coach because he grew up with a great coach. But he didn't just grow up with a great coach. He grew up with a great father. Coach Coburn wasn't asking anyone what made an effective coach. He knew, because he grew up watching one. And he wasn't asking anyone what made an effective father. He had seen one in action.

I wonder what kind of father Coach Sanders had? I can't say for sure, but I don't think he came from a long line of Puritans.

Not everyone has a coach like Coach Coburn; not everyone has a father like Coach Coburn had. If you did, you are one of the fortunate men on this planet. If you didn't, you have the opportunity of putting a new link in your family chain.

50 WAYS TO COACH YOUR CHILDREN

So where do you begin? And just exactly what does a coach do? Let me throw out fifty coaching tips that might help you get jump-started. Some of these are for younger kids and some are for older. You could definitely add to this list; it's just a starting point. But these are fifty tangible and concrete things that you can do. And it will make a difference.

1. Coach them how to pray.
2. Coach them that the most important book in all the world is the Bible—and that they should read it every day.
3. Coach them in how to buy a car by taking them with you the next time you buy one.
4. Coach them in how to use the library.
5. Coach them in how to stand up to a bully and defend themselves.
6. Coach your sons that men protect women.
7. Coach them about money—at least 10 percent to God, 10 percent to savings, live off the rest (and while they are under your roof, they can take 10 percent for spending money and bank the other 70 percent).
8. Coach them to never make a major purchase without thinking about it for *at least* twenty-four hours.
9. Coach them to dribble with their left hand.
10. Coach them ahead of time how to handle pornography.
11. Coach your daughters that there are two kinds of beauty—outside and inside—and that inside is more important to you and God.
12. Coach them to respect and obey authority—parents, teachers, police officers, etc.
13. Coach them to be kind to the kids at school whom other kids make fun of.
14. Coach them not to cheat on homework or tests.
15. Coach them to immediately return the money when they have been given too much change.
16. Coach them to do a job right—the first time.
17. Coach them to open the door for their mother.
18. Coach them to share their victories, joys, sorrows, defeats, and hurt with you. You do that, by the way, by listening.

19. Coach them to do what's right when no one else is around because Jesus is always around. And Jesus will reward them because they have character.
20. Coach them not to lie—before they get into the habit.
21. Coach them that some things are more important than sports—like Sunday worship.
22. Coach them to change their oil every 3,000 miles—and get your daughter a cell phone when she starts driving (trust me on this . . . you'll have a better quality of life).
23. Coach them to say no to movies that their friends, even their Christian friends, say yes to.
24. Coach your son to be a gentleman.
25. Coach your daughter to be a lady.
26. Coach your son to tie a tie and polish his shoes—before he's thirty.
27. Coach them that when you say no you mean no.
28. Coach them that it's pretty great to kiss your wife.
29. Coach them that their very best friend ever will always be Jesus.
30. Coach them to call home if they'll be late—and to keep the battery charged on the cell phone.
31. Coach them to stand alone.
32. Coach them that they aren't followers—they are leaders.
33. Coach them that it's better to be respected than popular.
34. Coach them that motherhood is the most important job in the world and definitely more important than a career.
35. Coach them that it's a father's job to provide for his family.
36. Coach them that God wants men to lead in the home and in the church.

37. Coach them to never give personal information to someone they don't know on the phone.
38. Coach them that even if they do make it to the NBA, they are going to have to do something else for the next forty years.
39. Coach them that good daddies hug and kiss but they also spank, and they make sure to hug and kiss after they spank.
40. Coach them to know what to look for in a husband.
41. Coach them to know what to look for in a wife.
42. Coach your daughter that both God and you think she is very, very, valuable—and she won't act cheap.
43. Coach your son to keep his hands off his date.
44. Coach them how to handle a checking account by letting them have one when they are in high school.
45. Coach them to love people and use things—instead of the other way around.
46. Coach them to measure twice—and saw once.
47. Coach them that Daddy will never leave Mommy.
48. Coach them that the narrow way is always the best way.
49. Coach them that there is nothing they could ever do that would make you stop loving them.
50. Coach them that there is nothing they could ever do that would make God stop loving them.

That ought to keep you busy for a while.

—4—

CONFUSED CHRISTIAN KIDS

"Rather than love, than money, than fame, give me truth."

—Henry David Thoreau

Josh McDowell recently did a study of more than 3,700 Christian young people in America. These kids came from thousands of churches in the United States and Canada. These are kids who attend Bible-believing churches. These are kids who go to Sunday school, youth meetings, and Bible studies every week. They describe their families as close and loving and consider their families to be very positive. These are Christian kids, the good kids. But as Josh puts it, "Large proportions of our youth—a majority of whom say they have made a personal commitment to Jesus Christ—are involved in inappropriate, immoral, even illegal behavior."[1]

- 74 percent say they are morally and spiritually confused.
- 55 percent have engaged in fondling breasts, genitals, and/or sexual intercourse by the time they are eighteen.
- 55 percent say they are looking for answers.

Remember, these aren't the bad kids at the local high school. These are the church kids. Eighty-four percent of these kids go to church and youth group every week. The survey revealed some sad things about their spiritual condition. In the last ninety days:

- 66 percent lied to a parent, teacher, or other adult.
- 59 percent lied to their peers.
- 45 percent watched MTV at least once a week.
- 36 percent cheated on an exam.
- 23 percent used a tobacco product.
- 20 percent intentionally tried to physically hurt someone.
- 12 percent had gotten drunk.
- 8 percent had used illegal, nonprescription drugs.
- 65 percent of these kids say that they pray daily.

And remember, that's just ninety days' worth. Here's what doesn't make sense. Two-thirds of these kids say that they pray daily. Obviously these kids are not against God; they are for God. They are seeking God. But many of them are deeply confused.

This generation of Christian kids knows about the Lord. So why are these good, well-meaning Christian kids having such a hard time living out their beliefs? Josh takes a pretty good pass at giving an explanation:

> I believe that one of the prime reasons this generation is setting new records for dishonesty, disrespect, sexual promiscuity, violence, suicide, and other pathologies, is because they have lost their moral underpinnings, their foundational belief in morality and truth have been eroded. . . .
>
> Our children are being raised in a society that has largely rejected the notions of truth and morality, a society that has somewhere lost the ability to decide what is true and

right. Truth has become a matter of taste; morality has been replaced by individual preference.[2]

Allow me to quote one more paragraph from Josh. He really hammers the nail into the coffin with this statement:

> As we examine our children's view about truth and morality, it is apparent that the foundations upon which many parents, pastors, and youth leaders attempt to build are crumbling. Traditional biblical concepts are eroding; a Judeo-Christian world view is being undermined. Most of our youth lack the most basic moral perspectives that previous generations took for granted. Many of our young people are struggling with the concept of truth and how they are to apply it to their own life and experience. Our kids are confused about what truth is and who defines it; they are uncertain about what truths are absolute and what makes them absolute. Consequently, they are making conditional decisions, choosing what seems to be the best alternative at the time, *without reference to any fundamental set of precepts or underlying principles to guide their behavior* (emphasis added).[3]

These Christian kids are confused about right and wrong. How can a kid who is growing up in a Christian home where the Bible is central be confused about right and wrong? Good question. Maybe someone assumed that they knew right from wrong. But that's the wrong assumption to make in this day and age.

That's the bad news: Christian kids are in trouble. The trouble comes from their surroundings. They are in trouble because they are being raised in a wilderness. A moral and spiritual wilderness. And when you are in a wilderness that you have never been in before, you are much better off if you have someone who is familiar with that wilderness. If you've got someone who knows the territory and knows the dangers, then your chances for survival in the wilderness go up dramatically. Someone who is familiar with the wilderness is called a guide. Someone who is familiar with the moral wilderness and who can lead a child through it is called a father.

Believe it or not, kids can survive in a moral wilderness even when a society has largely rejected the notions of truth and morality. Kids can even survive in a society that has lost the ability to decide what is true and right. They can even survive in a society where morality has been replaced by individual preference. How can they survive against such overwhelming odds?

They can survive if they have a father who *hasn't* rejected the notions of truth and morality, who *hasn't* lost the ability to decide what is true and right or replaced morality with his individual preference. They can survive if they have a father who loves the Lord his God with all his heart, with all his soul, and with all of his might. They can survive if they have a father who is building his life on bedrock. But they are not going to do well if they have a father who is trying to build on half sand and half rock.

BUILDING ON BEDROCK

You have two options as you build your family. You can build for the short term or you can build for the long term. At the conclusion of the Sermon on the Mount, the Lord Jesus Christ went straight to the heart of the matter:

> **Therefore whoever hears these sayings of Mine, and does them, I will liken him to a wise man who built his house on the rock: and the rain descended, the floods came, and the winds blew and beat on that house; and it did not fall, for it was founded on the rock. But everyone who hears these sayings of Mine, and does not do them, will be like**

**a foolish man who built his house on the sand: and the
rain descended, the floods came, and the winds blew and
beat on that house; and it fell. And great was its fall.**
(Matt. 7:24–27 NKJV)

Christian fathers don't build on sand. They build on
bedrock.

In the last year, I read two biographies of Joseph P. Kennedy.
Joe Kennedy had a dream and his dream was that all four
of his sons would become president of the United States. His
first son, Joe Jr., was tragically killed in World War II. His
second son, John, became the thirty-fifth president of the
United States and was assassinated in 1963. The third son,
Bobby, was gunned down in a Los Angeles hotel when he was
running for president. The fourth son, Ted, as you know, is
probably the most influential member of the United States
Senate. He recently led the charge in the Senate to legalize
marriage between homosexuals.

In 1936, Joseph P. Kennedy had everything. He was worth
millions. According to biographers, when others had been
wiped out in the depression, he made a fortune bootlegging
whiskey. He was one of the most powerful men in America.
He owned a major film studio and he would become the
United States ambassador to England. He was a man without morals. A Supreme Court justice referred to him as the
most evil man that he had ever known.[4]

Joe Kennedy had a far-reaching vision for his family. He
planned on reshaping the course of America through his four
boys. His sons were the *primary* focus of his life.

During a golf game in 1936, he was lining up a putt on an
exclusive golf course in Palm Beach, Florida. One of the men
in his foursome said, "So, Joe, what are you doing with yourself these days?" Without taking his eye off the ball, Joe
replied, "My work is my sons."[5]

Joe Kennedy had the vision to do something great through his sons that would affect our nation for at least one hundred years. All of his wealth and all of his power were devoted to that end. For a while, his dream was within reach. Joe Kennedy built a powerful and fabulously wealthy dynasty. He built lavish homes and he made visionary plans. But when the storms came, his house fell, and great was its fall.

Joe Kennedy made a big mistake. He built on sand. The titles of the two biographies on Joe Kennedy's life are pregnant with meaning. The first is titled *Sins of the Father;* the second is *Seeds of Destruction.*

How would you feel if you knew that at the end of your life two biographies would be written about you with those titles? That's not much of a legacy. That's what happens when a guy builds on sand.

Christian fathers don't build on sand. They build on rock. To be more precise, they build on bedrock. And the bedrock that Christian fathers anchor into is Deuteronomy 6:1–7. Let's look at it a few verses at a time:

> **Now this is the commandment, the statutes and the judgments which the LORD your God has commanded me to teach you, that you might do them in the land where you are going over to possess it, so that you and your son and your grandson might fear the LORD your God, to keep all His statutes and His commandments, which I command you, all the days of your life, and that your days may be prolonged.** (vv. 1–2)

Notice that these words were written to the fathers of Israel. And these fathers made up a new generation in Israel. Deuteronomy was written after Israel had wandered in the wilderness for forty years. When they came out of Egypt under Moses' leadership, they should have gone directly into the promised land. But they didn't. Only two of the twelve spies believed that God would give them victory over the powerful people who occupied the promised land. Because of their unbelief, Israel wandered for forty years.

Deuteronomy is written to the men who were little boys when the ten spies refused to trust God to give them the promised land. The little boys are now the fathers of Israel, and the fathers are the new generation. Every family is a small civilization. The Israelite fathers had a shot at building a new civilization that would honor and obey God. They would then tell the truth of God to their children so that their children could pass that truth on to the next generation in the family chain. What an amazing opportunity was before these fathers! They were going to go into the promised land under the leadership of Joshua. And Moses reminded them of the commandments of God, that they might *do* them when they got into their new homes.

Moses was referring to the whole Law and specifically to the Ten Commandments. Moses instructed the men of Israel to do and obey the Ten Commandments as they went into the new land to literally build a new civilization. The reason he emphasized the importance of obeying the Lord was that they were going to be surrounded by godless pagans. Do you remember all the "ites" in the Old Testament? The Canaanites, the Perizites, the Amorites, the Termites? All of these "ites" were in the promised land. And they were pagan people who worshiped sex. They murdered their children in "sacrifices," they were shot through with venereal disease because of their immorality, and they pierced their body parts as symbols of their freedom and independence. And the fathers of Israel were going to go in and establish godly homes with all of these people living around them.

That sounds kind of familiar, doesn't it? Christian fathers are attempting to raise their children in godly homes where the Ten Commandments are taught and kept. But we are surrounded by godless pagans who worship sex, abort children, spread venereal disease and AIDS through godless lifestyles, and pierce and tattoo their bodies as symbols of their personal freedom. Maybe this Deuteronomy stuff has something to say to us after all.

On to verse 3:

> **O Israel [or in our case, O America], you should listen and be careful to do it, that it may be well with you and that you may multiply greatly, just as the LORD, the God of your fathers, has promised you, in a land flowing with milk and honey.**

Remember, this is specifically addressed to the fathers of Israel. They are told to listen and to carefully do it. Do what? *Do* the Law, *obey* the Law. And if they do, God will pour out His blessing and favor on them with Niagara Falls–like consistency. God will bless these men with children and He will prosper them. Now there's a deal that's hard to beat. By the way, God is still making that deal with men who will take Him seriously. That's what I was trying to get across last month to the men who receive my newsletter (to receive our newsletter, call 1-800-MENLEAD):

> It's Friday morning. In a few hours I will board a plane to head for San Francisco where I will spend the weekend teaching a group of men who want to stand tall for Jesus Christ. Last Friday I got on a plane to go to Selma, Alabama, to speak to nearly a thousand men who want to follow Jesus Christ with their whole hearts. There is a big difference between San Francisco, California, and Selma, Alabama. Two different cities, two different cultures, and almost two different languages! But in spite of the differences, both cities have something in common—God's men are in both places.

I continue to be amazed at the work that God is doing among men across this nation. It doesn't matter if it is Alabama, California, Florida, Idaho, Hawaii, or Iowa. Visit any state in this nation, and there are remarkable signs that God is doing something fresh and new among His men. And what is this fresh work that God is doing? It is showing itself in many ways, but allow me to give you ten specific, concrete traits that I see God developing in Christian men across our nation:

1. God is developing men who will have no other gods before them.
2. God is developing men who will not make any graven images that they will bow before and serve.
3. God is developing men who will not take His name in vain.
4. God is developing men who will not allow themselves to become so busy at work that they will not take at least one day off to refresh and replenish their most important relationships.
5. God is developing men who honor their fathers and mothers and see it as their responsibility to help care for them as they reach their senior years.
6. God is developing men who have nothing to do with murder, whether it be a method of expressing rage and revenge or a procedure to take the life of precious unborn children.
7. God is developing men who will not commit adultery even though many around them are saying this is acceptable masculine behavior.
8. God is developing men who will not steal time, money, taxes, or possessions that do not belong to them.
9. God is developing men who will not bear false witness when they testify before a jury or when they

speak of a friend who is not present in the room. In other words, He is developing men who are not liars.

10. God is developing men who will not covet but who will be content with all of the remarkable blessings that the Creator has already put in their hands.

Recently a judge ordered that the Ten Commandments be removed from a courtroom in Alabama. The governor of Alabama promised that, if necessary, he would call out the National Guard to prevent the Ten Commandments from being removed from that state courtroom. Just yesterday, the House of Representatives overwhelmingly passed a nonbinding resolution stating that the display of the Ten Commandments in government offices is permissible. I'm sure that the controversy over the posting of the Ten Commandments will continue to rage in the days ahead.

No federal judge can prevent a man from loving God with all his heart, with all his soul, and with all his mind. Gentlemen, if we genuinely love God it is going to come out in our behavior. Jesus said, "If you love Me, you will keep My commandments." In every state of the Union, the Ten Commandments are under attack and ridicule. Let's post those Ten Commandments in our hearts and in our behavior. That's where those Ten Commandments will make the greatest impact.

Verse 4 nails down an issue that the men of Israel had to understand as they entered the promised land to build a new civilization: "Hear, O Israel! The LORD is our God, the LORD is one!"

The promised land was full of pagans who were religious. But they did not worship one god, they worshiped all kinds of gods. You could take your pick. We've got a lot of gods in America. Some men drive their gods and some men live in their gods. Some men wear their gods on their wrists and other men work out their gods two hours a day, every day, keeping their gods in top condition. Some men have opted for the god of power, or the god of money, or the god of lying to get what they want. Every person has a god.

Moses was reminding the fathers of Israel that in the midst of all of these gods, there is One, and only One, true God to whom no other god could be compared.[6] Moses was reminding these men of the first commandment:

> **You shall have no other gods before Me. You shall not make for yourself an idol, or any likeness of what is in heaven above or on the earth beneath or in the water under the earth. You shall not worship them or serve them; for I, the LORD your God, am a jealous God, visiting the iniquity of the fathers on the children, on the third and the fourth generations of those who hate Me, but showing lovingkindness to thousands, to those who love Me and keep My commandments.** (Ex. 20:3–6)

Over the years, I've had many fathers ask me the same question. It usually goes something like this: "Before I became a Christian, I did a lot of very bad things. I mean bad stuff. I slept around, I got girls pregnant, and then I would make them get abortions. Is God going to punish my children for all the bad stuff that I did?"

The answer is no. If you look at the verse closely, you will see that God only does that to "those who hate Me." Do you hate God? No. You love Him and you are in absolute awe of His amazing grace that forgave you and cleansed you from all of your past sin. God is not going to visit your past sin on your children, He is going to pour out His grace and forgiveness to thousands of people in your family chain just as He did for you. I say this reverently: The blood of Jesus has got you covered. And because you are so overwhelmed by what the Lord Jesus Christ has done for you, verse 5 describes your response to Him: "And you shall love the LORD your God with all your heart and with all your soul and with all your might."

What Moses was saying to the fathers of Israel is this: You can't love God halfheartedly. It's all or nothing. You either love Him or you don't. Either get in the ark or get off. There's no middle ground.

You cannot build a Christian family if you simply love God with half of your heart. You can't be divided and you can't be double-minded. Wasn't it James who said that a double-minded man is unstable in all of his ways? You can't build your house on half sand and half rock. It has to be one or the other. You either love God from your gut or you don't.

If you are going to teach your children about God, then you must love the Lord your God with all your heart and with all your soul and with all your might. H. L. Mencken said it best: "A man who knows a subject thoroughly, a man so soaked in it that he eats it, sleeps it, and dreams it—this man can always teach it with success."

If you attempt to teach your children about God without loving God yourself with everything you've got, believe me, they are going to figure that out. So if you don't love God with everything you have, then don't attempt to teach your kids about God. They would be better off discovering the truth about Him on their own than to learn it from a father who knew the truth, but didn't do the truth. Fathers who love God have a passion to practice what they teach.

To put it another way, every father is either self-centered or God-centered. And this is something you can't fake. You especially can't fake out your kids. Because they see what you are really like. According to Henry Blackaby, the God-centered man looks like this:

- His confidence is in God.
- His dependence is on God.

- His life is focused on God.
- He is humble before God (he prefers others over himself).
- He denies himself.
- He seeks first the kingdom of God and His righteousness.
- He seeks God's perspective in every circumstance.
- He pursues holy and godly living.[7]

Why don't you go over that list slowly one more time? How are you doing in these areas? Where is your ultimate confidence and dependence? What is your essential focus? How are you doing in your pursuit of godly living? Does your life really look any different from the lives of the people who work with you? You see, these are the essential questions that enable us to measure how closely we are walking with Christ. And that's what a Christian father does.

Matthew Henry's life certainly looked different from the lives of those around him. Or should I say the way he handled life was different. Matthew Henry wrote one of the great commentaries on the Bible. One day, as he was coming home from the city, he was robbed. He made the following notation in his diary:

Let me be thankful—
first, because I was never robbed before
second, because although they took my wallet they
*   did not take my life*
third, because although they took my all, it was not
*   much*
and fourth, because it was I who was robbed, not I
*   who robbed.*

Now that's a godly man. There's a man who can teach a child about God. There's a man who is building on bedrock.

It's no accident that the reason Matthew Henry was a mature man was that he loved God with his whole heart. There was nothing halfhearted about him. There should be nothing halfhearted about you either.

> **And these words, which I am commanding you today, shall be on your heart; and you shall teach them diligently to your sons and shall talk of them when you sit in your house and when you walk by the way and when you lie down and when you rise up.** (vv. 6–7)

There are three tips in these two verses for the man who wants to build on bedrock instead of sand.

First, to build on bedrock, *the Word of God is to be in a father's heart*. Christian fathers are men of the Book. They read Scripture, they meditate on Scripture, and they memorize Scripture. That's how you get the Word of God on your heart.

Have you ever worked on memorizing Scripture? You may be thinking, *I could never do that. I don't have a good memory, or I'm too busy.* Give me a break. You can do it, and quite frankly, you need to do it.

So how do you get started? You won't believe how easy it is to get started. Just call up the local Christian bookstore and ask them if they have the Navigator's Scripture verse packet. If they don't have it, ask them to order it. Get yourself a verse packet. It's designed to fit in your shirt pocket or pants pocket. It will take you through a planned, systematic approach that will have you memorizing Scripture in no time. Literally hundreds of thousands of people have used this little tool for over forty years. In six months, you will have more Scripture in your mind and heart than you would have ever believed.

And every time you put another Scripture into your mind, you are grabbing on to more bedrock. "Your word I have hidden in my heart, / That I might not sin against You" (Ps. 119:11 NKJV).

Second, to build on bedrock, *fathers are commanded to teach their sons and daughters the Word of God*. This is not optional, it is required. And fathers aren't just to teach, they are to diligently teach.

Wise fathers will read the Word of God to their children when their children are young. Wise fathers will make sure that they teach their children the Scriptures early. One of the best ways to do that is to read to your children before they go to bed.

Kids love bedtime stories. And kids don't want to go to bed. That's why they are always open for a story. But instead of reading to them about Mickey Mouse or Donald Duck, why not make good use of that time? Walt Disney never came up with anything to beat the story of Moses being hidden in the bulrushes or Daniel in the lions' den or Naaman the leper dipping in the Jordan seven times. Your kids need to hear the Word of God while they are young. And when you read the Scriptures to your children you are shaping their minds and you are shaping their thinking. There's something else you are shaping when you read the Scriptures to them. You are shaping their value system.

So get yourself *The Beginner's Bible, The Rhyme Bible*, or *Little Talks with God*. When I was about seven my mom and dad bought me a ten-volume set called *The Bible Story* by Arthur Maxwell. What a great set and what incredible pictures. That ten-volume set contained over four hundred stories from the Bible. Quite frankly, as a kid that gave me a biblical foundation I wouldn't trade for anything. I still have those books and they are just down the hall in my son's bedroom.

The early years, right on up until the age of seven, are critical years. But what about after seven? Should fathers still teach? Absolutely. But here is where we have to be creative. In our family, over the years I have done different things to teach my kids the Scriptures. I mentioned earlier that most of the things we tried didn't work. But here's one that did work.

One of the best things that we ever did was to designate one night a week as "family night." We would all get together and simply read through a book of the Bible as a family. Let's say that we were going to read the book of Esther. On family night, we would turn off the TV and get everyone downstairs with their Bibles. We would read just one chapter. And if a chapter has, for example, 27 verses, I would say, "Rachel, you read verses 1 to 9, John, you read verses 10 to 18, and Josh, why don't you read verses 19 to 27." The next week we would go on to the next chapter.

After finishing our reading we would talk about what we read. Some nights we had great discussions and other nights it was pretty bland. But that's the way it is. We kept plugging as a family and read through a number of books together. That's what Deuteronomy 6:7 calls "diligence."

We no longer have three children under the age of five. Now we have three teenagers. And when a child hits the teenage years, you want to begin the process of helping that teenager get into the Scriptures on his or her own. You should encourage teens to establish a daily time in the Word, either when they first get up or before they go to bed. Teenagers are in transition from being a child to becoming an adult. So they have to become self-starters in the Scriptures. And it's your job to get them started. Don't ask them to have a consistent time in the Word if you're not doing it. That's not going to fly.

But let me give you a strong word of caution. When it comes to getting into the Word and establishing spiritual disciplines, you want to *encourage* them but not *force* them.

If you force your children to have a quiet time, they are going to resent it. You should encourage it, but don't mandate it. And the reason you wouldn't force it is this—you want it to come from them.

You can't force a son to love God, but you can encourage him to love God. You can't force a daughter to choose God, but once again, you should be encouraging her to choose God.

Two of my children enjoy reading. One doesn't. And that's okay. It's just how he is wired. Now it stands to reason that the one who doesn't enjoy reading is going to have a more difficult time establishing a consistent time to read the Scriptures than the other two. So I have done a couple of things. I have gotten him a translation that is easier to understand. And I have rewarded him for times when he has consistently read the Scriptures. In other words, I will motivate him to read when he normally wouldn't by rewarding his efforts. I have absolutely no problem with that. But I can't do that for him the rest of his life. And I won't have to.

The best thing that I can do to encourage my children to be in the Word is to be in the Word myself. The consistent example of a father who makes the Word a priority in his life will eventually rub off on his children. And eventually, they will follow his lead. But don't force the issue. Live the issue.

There's a third tip for those who want to build on bedrock in Deuteronomy 6:6–7. When it says that a father is to "diligently teach," the word for "teach" carries with it the idea of "sharpening the mind." That root verb was used to describe the process of sharpening a sword for battle.

When a father teaches his children, he is sharpening his swords for spiritual battle. David actually refers to children in Psalm 127 as "arrows." But children are also individual swords who will fight the battle of truth in their generation. So they must be kept sharp.

Let me level with you. If you want your kids to be sharp spiritually, then *you* better be sharp spiritually. This is why you can't be halfhearted about following Christ. The halfhearted father is trying to build on sand and rock at the same time. And all that does is spiritually confuse his children.

A teenage girl recently wrote the following letter to *Brio,* a Christian magazine for teenage girls:

> Dear Susie:
>
> I need help. I can't handle this any longer.
>
> Today, I found a porno movie in my father's room. He is a pastor. I don't know what to think or what to do. I was gonna shrug it off but how?
>
> I also have a problem with guys. I don't know how or what happens, but I let them take advantage of me. I never go as far as actual sex but still. I feel bad saying no. Sometimes I can't even say it at all. I usually go for pretty decent guys but it doesn't matter . . . they're all the same. I've even tried going in groups; it doesn't help . . . we always end up alone. I do admit it's all my fault. I don't know what to do. I've tried everything.
>
> I found out my friend was gay . . . should I still be friends with him? I mean he's a nice guy . . . but aren't we suppose to shun that stuff?
>
> Sometimes I feel like dying. If someone does kill themselves, do they go to hell for it? And my other friends want to or tried to . . . would they go to hell? I heard you do. Is it true? And how do I get suicidal thoughts out of my head?[8]

Here is a Christian girl raised in a Christian home. A pastor's home. She is completely confused. She's confused about homosexuality and about her own sexuality. She is also suicidal and is confused about her eternal destination if she were to take her own life. I have a question and the question is this: What is the central issue of confusion in this girl's life? The answer is pretty clear. She has a father who is a pastor who hides porno films in his bedroom. That's the central reason this teenage girl is confused. She has a father who teaches truth but who doesn't do truth.

I'm sure that this father is concerned for his daughter and I'm sure that he must sense some of her confusion. I would imagine that he prays for his daughter. But in the words of Thomas Fuller, "none can pray well but he that lives well." This father needs to pray for himself. For he is the one who is confusing his daughter. He teaches one thing and does another. No wonder she is confused about what is right and wrong.

The essential qualification to teaching your children the truth of God is for you to love God with your whole heart. Our children desperately want to know if our faith is real. They want to know, "Does my dad really know God? In his heart of hearts, does he really believe?" That's a question that deserves an answer. And we answer it by our daily behavior.

A few weeks ago, I was in the car with my two boys. John is sixteen, and Josh is thirteen. We were stopped at a traffic light, waiting for it to turn green. As we waited, a woman who was obviously emotionally starved for attention crossed the street in front of us. How do I know that she was emotionally starved? By the way she was dressed and the way she carried herself. Let's put it this way. She was wearing the minimum. And she wanted every guy at the intersection to notice.

A few minutes later, John said, "You know what, Dad? You never look."

"Look at what?"

"You never look at women."

"How do you know I don't look at women?"

"Because I watch you all the time. I've watched you since I was a little boy. I've watched you on airplanes, I've watched you in restaurants, I've watched you at the beach, and I watched you back there at that intersection. And I have never seen you look. Not once. And I watch you constantly."

"Well, John, I saw that woman, and so did you. But you have to train yourself to look away immediately when you see someone like that."

"That's what I mean, Dad. You look away. And that's what you tell those guys at your conferences to do. I've heard you tell them that for years. That's why I watch you so closely. I want to see if you will do what you say a man should do."

"One of the reasons I look away is that I know you are watching me. That's why the real test of a man is his character instead of his reputation."

Then Josh jumped in and said, "Dad, reputation is what people think you are. But character is what you are when no one else is around. That's what you teach, Dad."

"That's right, Josh. Maybe John has never seen me look, but the real test is if I look when no one else is around. You see, God is always around. And He's looking for men who will obey Him when they're all by themselves."

I don't tell you that story because it makes me look good. The fact of the matter is that I have looked. But I am constantly working to discipline myself not to look. The reason I tell you that story is that it sent chills up my spine. My kids are constantly watching me, and your kids are constantly watching you.

I was fortunate enough to grow up with a father who taught the importance of sexual purity. I was also fortunate enough to have a father who *modeled* the importance of sexual purity. My dad didn't look. He showed me the truth. I'm simply passing it on to my sons so that they can pass it on to their boys. If you love God, you will begin to look away from sexual temptation. And if you look away, that will clear up any confusion your boys have about whether they should look away.

WHITE FANG

In Jack London's famous book *White Fang,* he tells the story of a dog that is half wolf, half dog. As a puppy, White Fang was treacherously abused by his cruel master. He was repeatedly kicked, beaten, and half starved. After several years of abuse, he found his way to a new master, Weeden Scott. In the story of White Fang there is a tremendous section where the wolf dog undergoes an amazing transformation from his old life to a new life. It's as though the great animal had a change of heart.

White Fang was very fond of chickens and on one occasion raided a chicken-roost and killed fifty hens. His master, Weeden Scott, whom White Fang saw as man-God and "loved with a single heart," scolded him and then took him into the chicken yard. When White Fang saw his favorite food walking around right in front of him he obeyed his natural impulse and lunged for a chicken. He was immediately checked by his master's voice. They stayed in the chicken yard for quite a while and every time White Fang made a move toward a chicken his master's voice would stop him. In this way he learned what his master wanted—he had learned to ignore the chickens.

Weeden Scott's father argued that you "couldn't cure a chicken killer," but Weeden challenged him and they agreed to lock White Fang in with the chickens all afternoon.[9]

> Locked in the yard and there deserted by the master, White Fang lay down and went to sleep. Once he got up and walked over to the trough of water. The chickens he calmly ignored. So far as he was concerned they did not exist. At four o'clock he executed a running jump, gained the roof of the chicken house and leaped to the ground outside, whence he sauntered gravely to the house. He had learned the law.[10]

Out of a love and desire to obey his master's will, White Fang overcame his natural, inborn desires. He may not have understood the reason, but he chose to bend his will to his master's.[11]

White Fang learned to love his new master, Weeden Scott, with all of his heart, with all of his soul, and with all of his might. He wasn't halfhearted toward his master. He followed his new master with everything that he had.

That's what children need to clear up the moral and spiritual confusion in their lives. They need a father to lead who isn't confused about whom he is serving. And they need a father who doesn't confuse them by trying to love God with half his heart or build on sand and rock at the same time.

Twenty-four years after Joe Kennedy lined up his putt and declared that "my work is my sons," his son John, the newly elected president of the United States, stood on that same golf course with Billy Graham. Mr. Graham tells it in his own words:

> Just a few days before president-elect John F. Kennedy was to be inaugurated, I was invited to join him and Senator George Smathers in Florida for a golf game and an evening visit at the Kennedy compound in Palm Beach. As we were driving back from the golf course, President Kennedy parked the car, turned to me and asked, "Do you believe Jesus Christ is coming back to earth again?" I was dumbfounded at his question. For one thing, I never dreamed that Mr. Kennedy would ask a question like that, and for another, I wasn't even sure that he knew Jesus was supposed to come back! Having only been with him a few times prior to that incident I had no grasp of his religious knowledge. "Yes sir, I do," I replied.
>
> "All right," he said. "Explain it to me." So for several minutes I had the opportunity to talk with him about the second coming of Jesus Christ.[12]

That was a great opportunity for Mr. Graham to explain to John F. Kennedy the truth about Jesus Christ.

John Kennedy as a boy was in church virtually every Sunday of his life. He had a father who gave large sums of money to their church. But when it came to Jesus Christ, John was very confused. And without question, a major contributor to his confusion about spiritual things was his father.

When John Kennedy was twelve years old, his father invited the then famous actress Gloria Swanson to join the family at their summer home. Unknown to his children, Joe Kennedy was having an affair with the actress. One afternoon, Joe decided to take Gloria out on the sailboat. Jack found out and hid below deck. When they were a couple of miles out to sea, Jack decided to come up and surprise them. He was horrified to come up on deck and see his father having sexual intercourse with Gloria Swanson. Stunned, shocked, and shamed by his father's behavior, he threw himself into the ocean to kill himself. His father quickly pulled him back to the boat.[13] No wonder he was confused about the truth.

Is your personal behavior confusing your kids about the truth?

Or is your personal behavior explaining the truth of Jesus Christ to your children?

The ball, my friend, is in your court.

—5—

NASCAR FATHERING

"Fatherhood is a career imposed on you without any inquiry as to your fitness."

—Adlai Stevenson

When a child is born into your home, you have just eighteen years to do the job of a father. Actually, you don't have that long. Anne Ortlund once noted that children are "wet cement." And a father has about seven years before the foundation that he is pouring into his child's life is set. After that, he is simply refining the foundational work that has already been done in the life of his child. I believe it was Saint Francis Xavier who said, "Give me the children until they are seven, and then you may have them for the rest of their lives."

If you only have eighteen years with your son or daughter under your roof, then time is critical. And using time wisely to build our children is one of the great challenges of fatherhood. To not use that eighteen years wisely is one of the great tragedies of a man's life. Charlie Hedges drives the point home:

I witnessed a sad event about ten years ago while attending a celebration to honor a man for twenty-five years of leadership in a major Christian organization. Part of the program was a slide show depicting the man's accomplishments and service all across the United States. The slides showed him in various cities and states, speaking, shaking hands, and being generally quite grand. Mixed in, as an attempt to commend his dedicated wife, were occasional slides of her and the kids, at home—without him. As the presentation continued, it became embarrassingly apparent that this great Christian leader was also an absentee husband and father.

At the conclusion of the slide show, it was the man's turn to do what he does best, to speak. I will never forget the moment he stepped up to the podium. He was in tears as he said, "I never really knew what a poor husband and father I have been." The event jolted me because I knew that all of us face the same temptation almost daily.[1]

Charlie is absolutely right. All of us fight the battle of spending adequate time with our families. We face incredible demands on our time; most of us could use a twenty-eight-hour day. It just doesn't seem that there is enough time to get everything done.

Fathers juggle a lot of balls. I saw a juggler one time on a street corner in San Francisco. This guy was incredible. He didn't juggle balls. He juggled a briefcase, a waffle iron, a set of keys, a basketball, a checkbook, and a flaming torch, all at the same time. When you think about it, that's fathering. You're juggling work, finances, recreation; you've got a couple of sets of keys to your office, your house, and your cars; you're coaching your son's or daughter's team, and on top of that, you've always got a fire to put out.

A wise old scribe by the name of Yelchaninov diagnosed the dilemma well:

> Our continual mistake is that we do not concentrate upon the present day, the actual hour, of our life; we live in the past or the future; we are continually expecting the coming of some special hour when our life shall unfold itself in its significance. And we do not observe that life is flowing like water through our fingers, sifting like precious grain from a loosely fastened bag.

In 1966, Peter Drucker wrote a book that challenged every businessman who read it. His book was titled *The Effective Executive*. It is a classic and it still sells thousands of copies each year. One of Drucker's key principles in his book was that "an effective executive knows where his time goes." So does an effective father. He watches his time carefully. Of course, he is juggling many responsibilities. But there is nothing more important in the life of a Christian father than his children. And since he only has eighteen years or so with those kids under his roof, he is very careful to make sure that he makes the most of that time before it is gone.

From 1934 to 1963, Alcatraz was the mother of all federal penitentiaries. Each incoming prisoner, when he was ushered into his cell, was given a copy of the Alcatraz rules and regulations. Rule number five outlined their rights: "You are entitled to food, clothing, shelter, and medical attention. Anything else you get is a privilege."

That rule makes sense in a prison. But it doesn't make any sense in a family. Most fathers would never make that statement to their children. But it is astonishing to see how many fathers actually father according to rule five of the Alcatraz rules and regulations. They give their children food, clothing, shelter, and medical attention. But they don't give them time. That's a privilege they keep to themselves.

In a recent interview published in the *Washington Times*, Yassir Arafat told about his personal difficulties in giving his daughter enough of his time. He was working early one morning at his office. There was a knock at the door, and one of his aides came in, holding in his arms a beautiful one-year-old little girl.

"Who is that child?" Arafat demanded.

After a moment of hesitation the aide replied with astonishment, "Sir, this is your daughter."[2]

That little girl in the story is not only Arafat's daughter, she is his *only* daughter. And he didn't have a clue who she was. That little girl had food, clothing, shelter, and medical attention. But she is going to need more than that from her father; she is going to need him. It is a father's responsibility to give time to his children. And to a child, time with his or her father is just as important as food, clothing, shelter, and medical care.

When I read that story about Arafat, I wasn't surprised. In the same article he admitted to referring to his wife as his second wife. Actually, she is his first wife. But Arafat refers to her as his second wife. And then he explains that his first wife is the Palestinian people.

Most men are not this crass and candid about the distractions that keep them from fulfilling their family responsibilities. And most fathers can at least recognize their children when they come into a room. But just because a man can recognize his children does not mean that he does not fight the battle of giving his children time. As Thomas Carlyle described it, "The greatest fault is to be conscious of none."

Children obviously need food, clothing, shelter, and medical attention. But they need more:

- They need their father's love.
- They need their father's wisdom.
- They need their father's concern.
- They need their father's discipline.

And the only way they are going to get those things is if they get something else. They need their father's time. But here is the rub. There is nothing more difficult for a father to give to his children than his time. A father can give his son money, he can give him a car, he can give him a college education. But what he needs is time. Your time. And plenty of it.

A group was going on a backcountry wilderness exploration in Canada. The people arrived at the outfitter's camp on the edge of the woods and spent the morning preparing packs and supplies for the long trek. But there was a problem. A member of the expedition noticed that the guide lacked maps for the backcountry they would explore.

No maps! To make matters worse, no compass! They anxiously approached the guide with their growing worry, but he looked confidently at them and smiled. "Maps and compasses are not the way through these mountains," he announced. "I am the way through the mountains."[3]

If you are a father, then you are the one to take your kids through the mountains. But if you are too busy at work, or are rarely at home and available, then your children are in major trouble. They need you and they need your time.

CHILDREN—A NECESSARY EVIL?

Many fathers, if not most fathers, are consumed by their work. Dr. Armand Nicholi of Harvard Medical School has been studying fathers and children for years. And he nails the national mind-set toward children:

> Our society, especially our institutions—schools, colleges, corporations, medical schools and hospitals—all seem to view the family as a necessary evil. The implication is that you spend a certain amount of time with your family because it's necessary to do so, but then you get back to the work that is really important.[4]

If you think that Dr. Nicholi is overstating the problem, you should know that he can back that statement up with the facts.

> The upshot of all these changes is that parents in this country spend less time with their children than in any other nation in the world, perhaps with the exception of England—the one country that surpasses the U.S. in violent crime and juvenile delinquency. Cross cultural studies show that even in countries where children are brought up in collectives, parents tend to spend more time with their children than they do in this country. Research shows that, in Russia, fathers spend as much as two and three hours a day with their children. But, in this country, according to a study out of Boston, fathers spend on the average about 37 seconds a day with their young children.[5]

Thirty-seven seconds a day. That's not a lot of time. But a lot of good men who love their kids have conned themselves into thinking that if they make the most of that short amount of time, they really are doing the job. But they're not. Fathering is a job you can't get done in thirty-seven seconds a day. It just isn't possible.

NASCAR FATHERS

Auto racing is a huge sport in the South. And it is coming to Dallas-Fort Worth where I live. In just a few weeks, the very first race at the Texas Motor Speedway will be held. They are already sold out. And on race day, close to 200,000 people will be in attendance.

The most amazing thing to me about a NASCAR race is not the race itself. The most amazing thing to me is the pit stops. The seven men who comprise the crew are incredible. When the driver pulls into the pit, those seven men jump over the retaining wall in complete unison. At the rear of the car, the gas-can man inserts the nozzle of an eighty-pound gas can into the gas tank. The catch-can man holds it in place as the gas-can man grabs a second can. At the exact same time, the jack man raises the right side of the car, so that the rear and front tire changers can get the lug nuts off. As soon as they get those lug nuts off, the tire carriers hand them the new tires, which they quickly put on. The jack man then raises the left side of the car, where the tires are changed by the same synchronized process. He then drops the car off the jack, thus signaling the driver to get out of the pit. These guys fill a twenty-two-gallon gas tank and change four tires in *eighteen* seconds. That is nothing short of amazing.

I have met some of the men who work in the pits at the NASCAR races. Many of them are Christians. But I will tell you a secret about these guys. They don't father the same way that they work a race. They know it takes more than an eighteen-second pit stop every evening to be a Christian father.

NASCAR fathers think they can father like that. Every Monday morning they start their engines and go roaring off on the fast track of work. Most days the race is so intense and competitive that they don't even make it home for dinner. But sometime after 7 or 8 that night they come roaring into the pits. These dads get out, say hi to their wives, gulp down supper, take a quick look at their daughter's report card, pat their son on the head, and say goodnight as the kids are going off to bed. And the average NASCAR father does it in thirty-seven seconds. Then he jumps into bed, catches some shut-eye, and gets up real early and gets back in the race before the kids ever get out of bed. That's NASCAR fathering. It doesn't work, but it's amazing how many Christian fathers think they can make it work.

I got a call this morning from a friend of mine who lives in another state. He's part of a small group of guys that I know who have been meeting together for several years. (I've changed the name and a few details to keep this guy anonymous.)

"So how is Dave?" I asked. "I haven't seen him for close to a year."

"Well, I think he's doing okay. I've only talked with him twice myself in the last six months."

"I thought you were in an accountability group together that met every week."

"Well, we were. But he has taken on so much responsibility at work that he has absolutely no time for anything else."

"He must be really putting in the hours if he's that loaded."

"Steve, my guess is that he is putting in eighty to ninety hours a week."

"How are things going at home for him?"

"You know that my wife and his wife are best friends. And although he says that everything is going fine at home, that's not what his wife says. He simply is never there."

Let me tell you about this guy. I know him fairly well. He is a very successful entrepreneur. He loves Jesus Christ with everything that he has, and he loves his wife and his kids. I know that he does because I've seen him shed tears of gratitude in a restaurant as he talked to me about his family.

This man is a Christian father if I've ever seen one. But right now, for some reason, he's become a NASCAR father. I don't think he realizes it, but he is seriously neglecting his kids. And not only are his kids crying out for his attention, but his wife is too. Why can't he see this? Everyone else around him can see it.

Not only does he not have time for his family, he doesn't have time for anybody . . . including his friends. His real friends—the guys who have always shot straight with him.

But he has distanced and isolated himself. George Swinnock said it best: "Satan watches for those vessels that sail without a convoy."

I'm sure Dave views himself as doing an effective job at work. But anyone consistently working eighty hours a week could hardly qualify as an "effective" executive. He may be a busy executive but that doesn't mean that he is effective. And it certainly makes his effectiveness as a father highly suspect.

The best I can figure, about a year ago he got conned into making some bad decisions about his time and his commitments on the job. And he is now the classic illustration of a NASCAR father. He may not think so but with his putting in eighty hours a week he'll be lucky if his kids see him when he makes a pit stop. If he would slow down and listen to the messages that are coming to him from his wife and his kids he would quickly pick up that they are starving for his attention. But he is just too busy to hear them. And he keeps digging himself deeper. I just hope he sees it before somebody throws a banquet to honor him for twenty-five years of service to his company.

The enemy loves to take Christian fathers and get their careers out of balance. He tends to do this with those who are highly motivated and self-starters—guys who want to do a job and do it right. Those are all great traits. But they are also traits that can quietly lead men into distraction from their central responsibilities as Christian fathers. And that's why the enemy loves to take people like this and distract them. When a guy gets distracted, he gets distanced. Here's an ironclad fathering formula that you can take to the bank:

Distraction always creates distance; distance is toxic to Christian fathers.

Physical distance from your children is toxic; emotional distance from your children is even more toxic.

Winston Churchill was sent away by his parents to boarding school at the age of seven. He rarely, if ever, had contact with his father, Lord Randolph, who showed very little interest in spending time with his young son. And that devastated Winston.

> Like most schoolchildren separated from their families, Winston called repeatedly for visits from his parents . . . for the most part his cries went unanswered. Lord Randolph, by now fully engaged in politics, would not modify his crowded schedule for the sake of his son . . . (Winston's) efforts to draw closer to his father, to gain his confidence, to strike an intimate note, to relate to him in a warm and meaningful way, as a father and son should, were met by a blank wall of indifference that must have seemed incomprehensible to a young child.[6]

Years later, Churchill wrote about the agony of a childhood separated from his father. Although his father never came to visit him at school, he looked forward to going home for the holidays. More often than not, when he arrived home, he found that his father was gone. Both his father and mother were "away" for the holidays. As a boy, Winston usually spent his holiday time at "home" with a hired nanny. His dad was just too busy.

Earlier this evening, I caught a very short segment of an interview with a former prisoner of war in Vietnam. This man was in the Hanoi Hilton for six and a half years. The interviewer was asking him about the price he paid in being separated from his family for so long. His response was that both he and his family had "time scars."

In his own words, he said,

> I can never make up those six years. I can never make up those six years that I missed in my son's life. I missed the

years in his life between the ages of two and eight. I can
never get those years back. I can never go back to my
daughter's high school years. I can never see her cheerleading at a football game. I can never make that up to her.
And when I think of all that I have missed, and can never
recover, well, those are what we refer to as time scars.

This father *couldn't* be with his children for six years. And
he missed an incredible amount of their lives. What is even
more tragic is when a father *could* be there and isn't. That's
when the time scars go real deep. It's one thing to know your
father won't be at a ball game because he is a prisoner of war
halfway around the world. It's another to know that he won't
be there because he's working late again at his office just ten
miles down the freeway.

Let's go back to my friend for a minute. The reason that
I'm so concerned about him is that with his eighty-hour
workweek he is creating in his children the same resentment
that Lord Randolph created in young Winston. And I know
that he doesn't realize it. But it is inevitable. Children who
are cheated from the time that they need with their father
will become resentful. You can count on it. And that is a very
painful price to pay. Both the child and the father will carry
deep time scars for the rest of their lives.

So what has happened to my friend? Does this guy *want* to
be distanced from his wife? No. Does he *want* to be distanced
from his kids? Absolutely not. But that's exactly where he is.
They all live under the same roof, but the way things are right
now, this guy might as well be in Zimbabwe. His family feels
as though he is away every day, except for the holidays.

So what happened? What caused the distraction that led
to the distance? Is he involved with another woman? No. Is
he embezzling money from his company? No. He simply
committed himself to more responsibility than he could legitimately handle. Although the workload is challenging and

rewarding, it is simply too much. He is paying a very high price for self-fulfillment.

Don't misunderstand me. The Christian father works, and he works hard.

- Work is necessary.
- Work is biblical.
- Work is important.

The Christian father does his work, no matter what kind of work it is, to the glory of God. Whatever work you do, you should do it to the very best of your ability.

That's why I have always appreciated the wise counsel of John Ruskin. Over one hundred years ago, he wrote this prescription for work: "In order that people may be happy in their work, these three things are needed: they must be fit for it, they must have a sense of success in it, and they must not do too much of it."

If you are cut out for your work, and you have a sense of success in your work, then you are going to struggle with doing too much work. The guy who doesn't enjoy his work has always got one eye on the clock. He counts the hours and minutes until quittin' time. But if you enjoy your work, the hours fly by! And you are a father who must be very, very careful with your time. Let's be gut-level honest about this. The man who enjoys his work and is successful at work is going to have a hard time leaving his work. The temptation for fathers who love what they are doing is to spend too much time doing what they love to do.

My entrepreneurial friend loves his work. He is very, very good at what he does, and success has come his way as a result of the quality of work that he puts out. But another result is that he has become as addicted to his work as the guy smoking crack in some back alley. It's a different kind of addiction, but it's just as devastating to his family.

This is not a chapter on work. It's a chapter on the absolute importance of giving our children the time that they need to develop into godly men and women. But we have to talk for a minute about work because so often it is a distorted view of work that keeps us from giving our children the time with us that they so desperately need.

William Beausay has written an excellent book on fathering boys. It is appropriately titled *Boys!* He gives some great advice to fathers:

> It is your job to be steadfast and unchanging through the swirling waters of boyhood. Your boy is depending on you to maintain a sensible course in life and model temperance, sensibility, and stability because he has little or none.
>
> I did consulting a few years back with some professional water-skiers. These folks aren't content to stay tucked neatly and safely behind a nice little boat. They slash and bang, looking for wakes to pound, ramps to fly off, and danger to sneer at! They have no sense of fear, no obvious concern of personal safety. They're just like boys. The only thing steady in a water-skier's life is the boat.
>
> Consider yourself the boat your son skis behind. He may act out of control, but he depends on you to stay the course and show him where to go. Your son will go where you pull him.[7]

But what if you're not ever around to pull your son? Then what is he going to do? What if you are a guy who has never come to grips with being a workaholic? What is that lack of time going to do to your son or daughter? I'll tell you what it's going to do. It's going to devastate the child. That's why we have to have a grip on our time.

Why do we work? If I were a betting man I'd put down money that only one out of ten guys has really thought this one through. When all is said and done, why does a guy get up and go to work in the first place?

- Some men get up and go to work because their work is a perfect match for their skills and abilities. These guys can't wait to get to the office or shop.
- Some men get up and go to work because they are enjoying a great deal of success at their jobs. They are good at what they do and they are compensated well. That's why they get up every morning.
- Some men get up and go to work because they are trying to climb the corporate ladder.
- Some men get up and go to work because they are highly motivated to succeed in a new business that they have started.
- Some men get up and go to work because they want to be successful and acquire a bigger house, a nicer car, and a membership in the country club.

Ultimately, the real reason that a father goes to work is that he is responsible to provide for his children. And when everything else is stripped away, that's really the gut-level motivation.

Just yesterday I ran into an acquaintance I hadn't seen in close to a year. We were both waiting for our wives to come out of the same meeting. As we were making small talk, I said, "How's business these days?"

Have you ever been in a dentist's chair and suddenly, as he's poking around in your mouth, he hits a nerve? That's what I did unintentionally to this guy. I hit a nerve.

He looked at me and there was great sadness in his eyes.

"Steve, I lost my business about three months ago. I've been completely wiped out. I have lost everything. I'm driving a delivery truck just trying to keep a roof over our heads and buy groceries. It's all I can do right now to provide for my family."

This guy had done pretty well. He has four teenagers. He was making a very good income. Nice house. Nice cars. But it was suddenly all stripped away. I don't know all of the circumstances since we just had a few minutes to talk. But suffice it to say that the central reason this guy is getting up and going to work every morning is to provide for his children. And right now, he knows that's the reason he gets up every morning to do a job that he's overqualified to do. The bottom line is provision.

He used to have a job that fit his skills and interests. Now he doesn't. He used to have a job that rewarded him with a fair amount of success. Now he doesn't. So why does this father get up and go to work every day? He goes to a job that he doesn't particularly enjoy and that doesn't offer much success because he has a family to provide for. When you strip all of the varnish off, that's why we fathers do what we do—for our kids.

Wise fathers understand that they must devote significant hours of every day to providing for their children. But wise fathers also refuse to pour all of their energies into their work, for that would keep them from their most important work.

The absolute, bottom-line reason that fathers go to work is to provide for their families. Provision is our job.

And if a guy doesn't get up and provide for his family, the Scriptures say that "if anyone does not provide for his own, and especially for those of his household, he has denied the faith and is worse than an unbeliever" (1 Tim. 5:8 NKJV).

I see a principle here and the principle is this: *Our work is not to distract us from our children, our work is to provide for our children.* But if we are not careful our work can become a substitute for our children. In other words, gentlemen, our work is *for* our children. It is not to be a distraction that keeps us from our children.

The reason that you go to work is to provide for your children, who are your ultimate work. Our culture has it reversed. The focus of a father's life is not his career. The focus of a man's life is his children. And we get up and go to work so that we can provide for the physical needs of our children.

But I am also to provide for the *emotional* needs of my children. And I am also to provide for their *spiritual* needs. Emotional needs and spiritual needs don't require money. They require time. Large doses of time.

Most of us fathers talk to our kids about the importance of resisting peer pressure. But I have noticed that peer pressure doesn't end when you get out of high school or college. There is peer pressure in your twenties and their is peer pressure in your thirties. As a matter of fact, peer pressure never goes away.

Most of our peers are going the wrong direction. And the pressure that we all face is to go along with them. But Jesus said, "The way is broad that leads to destruction" (Matt. 7:13). That's the way the majority of our peers are heading. Let's face it, guys. Most of our peers are screwed up. The reason a lot of them are successful is that they are total and absolute failures on the home front. Not all of them, but most of them. So why should I let them pressure me? I don't want to be like them and neither do you. They are going the wrong way with their careers. They are going the wrong way with their marriages. They are going the wrong way with their children. They are going the wrong way with their time.

I refuse to give in to that pressure. I've only got eighteen years with my kids. I've got eighteen years to see my little girl become a godly woman (and by the time this book is in your hands my eighteen years with my "little girl" at home will be over and she will be away at college). I've only got eighteen years to see my two boys become godly men who know how to follow Christ. And if I've only got eighteen years with them before I release them into the world, then I'm going to think long and hard before I give up any of that time to the pressure of my screwed-up peers who can't keep their marriages or their kids together. I'm sorry, but life is too short. And my kids are too precious.

Yes, I work hard. Yes, it's my job to bring home the bacon. But I also have to be smart enough to know when it's time to turn it off so I can get home and be a father. I need to be smart enough to know when to say no to a promotion, because when I really look at it from all the angles and weigh it in light of my family responsibilities it comes out as a demotion. Very few of your peers have what it takes to make those kinds of insightful decisions. But the good fathers do. And God will honor them for it.

We must set limits on our work. If we don't, it has the potential to not only distract us, but to consume us.

So let me throw out a question. How are you doing on being distracted from your fathering responsibilities? To be honest, you are probably the wrong person to ask. Most of us tend to rate ourselves a little too highly.

Let me offer what could be an uncomfortable suggestion. If you really want to know how you are doing on distraction and distance, why don't you ask your wife? Get a baby-sitter for one night and take her out to dinner. You say you're too busy to do that? Then you just answered the question. If you find it difficult to find a night when the two of you can go talk, then take it from me. You've got a full-blown case of NASCAR fathering.

Here's what you do. You schedule the night, you find a baby-sitter, and you go to a place where you can talk. If the waiters are standing on the tables doing the Macarena, that's probably not your spot. And after you've had a nice dinner then pop the question. Get her up to speed by letting her know that you've been kicking around some ideas on distracted fathers. And that you don't want to be either a distracted father or a distracted husband. And then ask her how you're doing.

This is the time for you not to talk or interrupt. This is the time for you to listen. And you need to listen big-time. There's one other thing. And this is big; in fact, it's huge. Whatever you do, don't be defensive. If she starts to tell you that you have been distracted and that you have been distanced, whatever you do don't start defending yourself. Don't do it with your words and don't do it with your body language. And if you find yourself starting to get defensive, then you jump up on the table and do the Macarena. Do anything else but don't be defensive. Listen. Listen with your mind and listen with your heart. And take it like a man. God will see your openness and as a result, He will pour His favor upon your life. That's what Proverbs 19:20 means: "Listen to counsel and accept discipline, / That you may be wise the rest of your days."

Now here's the good part. She will love you for asking. And she will love you even more for listening. And if you're not defensive, well, let's just say that this could be one of the all-time great nights of your life. If you get my drift.

But that's not why you are asking the question. You are asking the question so that you can be the father you want to be. And while you're at it, ask her one more thing. Ask her to critique how you are doing with each of your kids. Ask her to give you her read on how each of your children is doing. Is there something specific she can tell you about each child that would enable you to close any distance that's developed? If you ask those two questions, you two will be off and running. And even as you are talking you are defeating the enemy. How are you defeating the enemy? When you are listening to your wife with your full and undivided attention, then you have just eliminated yourself from the ranks of NASCAR fathers.

When a father is making thirty-seven-second pit stops, he loses his influence. And when you lose your influence, you have given up your opportunity to anchor your children and their children.

When a father makes thirty-seven-second pit stops, his children become vulnerable. They become vulnerable to wrong influences, wrong friends, wrong thinking, and wrong behavior.

Someone is going to influence your children. It had better be you.

Most NASCAR fathers would never think to ask these questions. Number one they don't have the time, and number two it sounds too threatening. But Christian fathers will ask. And Christian fathers will listen and won't be defensive. A Christian father will take the information, digest it, and make the appropriate and necessary midcourse corrections. That's why your kids are so fortunate to have a man like you as their father.

As a result of your interaction with your wife, you can take three steps:

1. Calculate your time.

   - With your wife's input, decide how many hours you will put into work each week. What time will you leave the house? What time will you get home?
   - How many evenings will you be at home with your family?
   - Will you take the weekends off?
   - Will you be home for dinner?

2.   Control your time.

- Say yes to activities that include your children—like coaching and teaching Sunday school.

3.   Capture your time.

- Beware of too many family activities. There are many families in our community with children playing basketball, soccer, and baseball . . . at the same time. And I'm talking about the same child playing on three teams at once. I love sports, but that's crazy. There are other things in life besides going to games and practices every night. I refuse to let other out-of-balance fathers set the pace for me.
- Beware of too many church activities. This one may surprise you but it's possible to be at the church every single night. We have a great church, but I don't want to be there every night. You don't need to be there every night; and, if your pastor is in balance, he won't want you to be there every night. How do you know if your pastor is in balance? He won't be there every night.

Someone has said that the job of a father is to raise child-raisers. The goal of a father with a two-year-old son is to train that little boy in such a sterling way that in thirty years, that two-year-old will be a model father for his two-year-old. Fathering is demanding and fathering is daily. It's reading stories, changing diapers, bringing home a paycheck, coaching Little League, and saying no and meaning no. There are dozens of small tasks that make up a father's daily interaction with his children. But the wise father never forgets that the way he handles those small tasks of fathering will have enormous consequences for the next seventy years of his child's life. You are not just raising a child today. You are raising a future father, a future mother, a future grandfather, a future grandmother.

Michelangelo spent over four years of his life on his back painting the Sistine Chapel. Each day he would take a section of the ceiling, perhaps just several inches in diameter, and spend ten to twelve hours working on that very small and compact surface. The next day he would move to another small section. He did that every day for four and a half years. As he worked on the small tasks he never lost sight of the big picture. He never forgot his vision. And that's what kept him going as he did his tedious work. When he was done he had a masterpiece that is still admired four hundred years later.

That's the way a biblical father approaches fathering. He fathers every day in the situations that seem tiny, small, and insignificant. But those daily "fatherings" will all add up. And, with God's help, the father who takes his fathering seriously, and who takes his time seriously can produce a godly masterpiece that will be admired and appreciated for generations.

—6—
TAMING YOUR BARBARIANS

"We ought as much to pray for a bless-ing on our daily rod as upon our daily bread."

—John Owen

George Barna is no extremist. George Barna is the George Gallup of the evangelical Christian world. He is constantly polling people across America to get the pulse of what's going on in our nation. And he reports that information to Christian leaders throughout the country.

Barna was recently speaking to a group of Christian leaders in Nashville. Barna, who is not given to wild-eyed predictions or sensational statements, said something that sobered his audience. What he said was that in his opinion, in the next five to ten years, America is headed for either anarchy or revival.[1]

The *Oxford American Dictionary* defines *anarchy* as "the absence of government or control, resulting in lawlessness." And unless Almighty God intervenes, that's where we are going.

Anarchy in a nation begins as anarchy in the home. There are numerous homes in America, countless homes in America, where there is the absence of government, or control by fathers, resulting in lawlessness. Fundamentally, when you get right down to it, the soaring crime rate is a "father" issue.

I have a file sitting on my desk that is over one inch thick. In it are articles and news clippings that I have assembled over the last twelve months on crime. But I need to be more specific. It's not just a folder on crime. It's a folder on teenage crime. Allow me to give you a handful of excerpts. By the way, my purpose is not to overwhelm you with statistics on crime. My purpose is to underscore for you the importance of disciplining your own children.

Maybe you saw the cover story of *U.S. News and World Report* that was headlined, "Teenage Time Bombs: Violent Teenage Crime Is Soaring—And It's Going to Get Worse."

> The stories flicker on the screen with numbing repetition. In Chicago, two boys—one 12, one 13—are sentenced to prison after dropping a 5-year-old out of a 14th story window because he wouldn't steal candy for them. In New York, two teenage boys and a young woman lock up a 13-year old girl, repeatedly rape and torture her, then hang her up in a closet by her heels before she manages to escape. . . .
>
> We hear these tales so often now that we are beginning to accept them as a permanent way of life. . . . Evidence grows that we are spawning a new class of "super-predators" who threaten far more mayhem in the next few years. Chuck Colson has visited 600 prisons over the past two decades as leader of the Prison Fellowship Ministries. He writes in the *Wall Street Journal* that he has been "chilled to the bone" by his recent encounters with teenage prisoners. "Some were cold, distant, as if life had been sucked out; others were seething with rage and anger. An assistant warden at the Indiana State Penitentiary told Colson his biggest demand from older inmates is to be

protected from 19- and 20-year old kids. Since the juvenile population will grow considerably by the year 2000, there is serious danger that kids will soon be roaming urban neighborhoods like "teenage wolf packs."[2]

John Dilulio has had the same experience as Colson. Dilulio, who teaches at Princeton, recently wrote an article in Focus on the Family's *Citizen* magazine. It was titled, "Kids Who Scare Cops." Dilulio writes:

We're not just talking teenagers. . . . We're talking about boys whose voices have yet to change. We're talking about elementary-school youngsters who pack guns instead of lunches. We're talking about kids who have absolutely no respect for human life and no sense of the future. In short, we're talking big trouble that hasn't yet begun to crest. . . .

To cite just a few examples, following my May 1995 address to the district attorneys association, big-city prosecutors inundated me with war stories about the ever growing numbers of hardened, remorseless juveniles who were showing up in the system.

"They kill or maim on impulse, without any intelligible motive," said one. Likewise, a veteran beat policeman confided: "I never used to be scared. Now . . . every time I get a call involving juveniles, I pray I go home in one piece to my own kids."

To add my own observations to the pile, since 1980 I've studied persons and jails all over the country—San Quentin, Leavenworth, Rikers Island. I've been on the scene at prison murders and riots (and once I was almost killed inside a prison).

Moreover, I grew up in a pretty tough neighborhood and am built like an aging linebacker. I will still waltz backward, notebook in hand and alone, into any adult maximum-security cell block full of killers, rapists and muggers.

But a few years ago, I forswore research inside juvenile lock-ups. The buzz of impulsive violence, the vacant
stares and smiles, and the remorseless eyes were at once
too frightening and too depressing (my God, these are children!) for me to pretend to "study" them.[3]

But it's not just teenagers anymore. I have a story in my
file from the June 10, 1996, *Washington Times,* with the
headline: "Criminal justice system faced with rash of toddler
thugs."

We are now moving from teenagers to toddlers. This particular article mentions two separate incidents, one in Colorado and one in California, where a ten-year-old boy and a
six-year-old boy both beat infants to death. And the article
indicates that toddler thugs are becoming a problem all over
the nation.

Let's be very honest here. The tendency is to think that
this teenage crime problem is pretty much restricted to
the inner cities of our nation. And that it is a problem primarily among the black community. But that's not quite
right. The assistant attorney general of Arizona, Andrew Peyton Thomas, recently wrote that in Maricopa County, where
Phoenix is located, close to 40 percent of white teenage males
under the age of eighteen have been charged with a crime.[4]
That is a staggering statistic. The crime rate among white
juveniles is now growing twice as fast as among blacks.

Dan Korem, author of *Suburban Gangs—The Affluent
Rebels,* writes: "For the first time in U.S. history, kids from
affluent homes are forming their own deadly gangs in sub-
urbs and upscale communities in growing numbers. The
same terrifying trend is presenting itself across Europe, from
England to Switzerland and to Hungary."[5]

So what does fathering have to do with this? Just about
everything. A recent study indicated that "the best pre-
dictor of violent crime in a neighborhood is the proportion

of households without fathers."[6] Fathers, or rather the absence of them, have everything to do with kids who are out of control.

George Barna is reading the information correctly. We're on our way to anarchy. We have teenagers who are out of control, and kids in elementary school who are already committing violence without feeling anything in their consciences. But we have always been on the way to anarchy. That's really nothing new.

> When it comes to rearing children, every society is only twenty years away from barbarism. Twenty years is all we have to accomplish the task of civilizing the infants who are born into our midst each year. These savages know nothing of our language, our culture, our religion, our values, our customs. . . . The infant is totally ignorant about communism, fascism, democracy, civil liberties . . . respect, decency, honesty, customs, conventions, and manners. The barbarian must be tamed if civilization is to survive.[7]

BARBARIAN? MY DAUGHTER? MY SON? YOU BET

Gentlemen, there seems to be something that our culture is missing. Our culture is blind to a fundamental truth. You have a sin nature. I have a sin nature. And our children have a sin nature.

"All have sinned and fall short of the glory of God," we are told by the apostle Paul in Romans 3:23 (NKJV). But this sin problem is not one that can be resolved by changing our environment. It is a problem of the heart. And according to the Scriptures, our hearts are in pretty bad shape:

> *There is none righteous, not even one;*
> *There is none who understands,*

There is none who seeks for God;
All have turned aside, together they have become useless;
There is none who does good,
There is not even one.
Their throat is an open grave,
With their tongues they keep deceiving,
The poison of asps is under their lips;
Whose mouth is full of cursing and bitterness;
Their feet are swift to shed blood,
Destruction and misery are in their paths,
And the path of peace have they not known.
There is no fear of God before their eyes. (Rom. 3:10–18)

This is not a description of some far-off uncivilized nation. This is a description of *all* mankind, separated from God and trapped in moral depravity. This is you and I. And this is our children.

The Bible says that we are all born with the potential to become barbarians. And the first answer to the growing crime problem in America comes in recognizing this truth. If our children are to become happy and healthy adults, we've got to tame the barbaric nature that resides within them.

So who is going to tame and civilize these incredibly cute but potentially lethal barbarians? God expects fathers to do that. You tame your barbarians and I tame mine.

How does a father take a newborn child and keep him from becoming a barbarian twenty years down the line?

Notice what God said to the men of Israel:

> Now this is the commandment, the statutes and the judg-
> ments which the LORD your God has commanded me to
> teach you, that you might do them in the land where you
> are going over to possess it, *so that you and your son and
> your grandson might fear the LORD your God*, to keep all
> His statutes and His commandments, which I command

you, all the days of your life, and that your days may be prolonged. (Deut. 6:1–2, emphasis added)

Did you notice the effect that God's commandments were to have on Israel? They were meant to create within the fathers, and their sons, and their grandsons, a healthy "fear [of] the LORD."

THE SAFETY NET OF FEAR

The fear of the Lord is the glue that holds a society together. The fear of the Lord is the safety net that keeps a nation from falling into anarchy and chaos. And unfortunately, for the most part, we have lost the fear of the Lord in our nation.

The story is told of a public school teacher who was retiring early. When asked why, she responded:

> The problem is really fear. The teachers are now afraid of the principals. The principals are afraid of the superintendents. The superintendents are afraid of the school boards. The boards are afraid of the parents. And the parents are afraid of the children. But the children? They're not afraid of anybody.[8]

And that is precisely the problem. You dare not lose the fear of the Lord in your home. So what is the "fear of the Lord"?

The book of Proverbs mentions the fear of the Lord fourteen times. Among the references are the following:

- "The fear of the LORD is the beginning of knowledge." (1:7)
- "The fear of the LORD is the beginning of wisdom." (9:10)
- "The fear of the LORD prolongs life." (10:27)
- "In the fear of the LORD there is strong confidence." (14:26)
- "The fear of the LORD is a fountain of life." (14:27)

- "The fear of the LORD is the instruction for wisdom." (15:33)
- "By the fear of the LORD one keeps away from evil." (16:6)
- "The fear of the LORD leads to life." (19:23)

I like the way Proverbs 8:13 sums it all up: "The fear of the LORD is to hate evil."

In Deuteronomy 6, fathers are instructed to *teach their children the fear of the Lord*. The critical question is this. How does a child learn the fear of the Lord? This may surprise you, but a child learns the fear of the Lord by first experiencing the fear of a father.

Children should "fear" their fathers? Yes, they should, in the biblical sense. And the reason is this. If a child never learns to "fear" his earthly father, then how is he ever going to learn to "fear" his heavenly Father?

Here is a great answer to the question, What place should fear occupy in a child's attitude toward his mother or father?

> There is a narrow difference between acceptable, healthy "awe" and destructive fear. A child should have a general apprehension about the consequences of defying his parents. By contrast, he should not lie awake at night worrying about parental harshness or hostility. Perhaps a crude example will illustrate the difference between these aspects of fear. A busy highway can be a dangerous place to take a walk. In fact, it would be suicidal to stroll down the fast lane of a freeway at 6 p.m. on any Friday. I would not be so foolish as to get my exercise in that manner because I have a healthy fear of fast-moving automobiles. As long as I don't behave ridiculously, I have no cause for alarm. I am unthreatened by this source of danger because it only reacts to my willful defiance. I want my child to view me with the same healthy regard. As long as he does not choose to challenge me, openly and willfully, he lives in total safety. He need not duck and flinch when I suddenly scratch my

eyebrow. He should have no fear that I will ridicule him or treat him unkindly. He can enjoy complete security and safety—until he chooses to defy me. Then he'll have to face the consequences. This concept of fear which is better labeled "awe" is modeled after God's relationship with man; "The fear of God is the beginning of wisdom," we are taught. He is a God of wrath, and at the same time, a God of infinite love and mercy. These attributes are complementary, and should be represented in lesser degree in our homes.[9]

The "fear of the Lord" referred to in Scripture is a reverential awe that makes us want to live in obedience to God. And the fear of a father is a reverential awe that makes a child want to live in obedience to her father.

My dad understood this well. The previous quote spoke of a general apprehension about the consequences of defying a parent. Well, I had a very specific apprehension of defying my father. I am the oldest of three brothers. And we all had a very specific apprehension of defying my father (or worse, defying my mother; if my dad would find out about that, we were in double trouble).

Make no mistake about it. We had a lot of fun with our dad. And we knew that our dad loved us. We didn't quiver when he walked into the room, or fear that he might lose control. He didn't beat us and he didn't go into rages. He was very much in control; he just meant what he said. And if you didn't do what he said, there were consequences. Let's call them "meaningful consequences." And these "meaningful consequences" had the effect of making you avoid that same behavior in the future.

I cannot tell you how many times in high school some of my buddies would be getting ready to go out and create anonymous havoc. They would always ask me to go along, and I would decline. I just knew that somehow, some way, in his "omniscience" and "all-knowing" ability, my dad would find out. And that's why I didn't go. It just wasn't worth it. I was sixteen. And I wanted to live to be seventeen!

Proverbs 10:27 says that the fear of the Lord prolongs life. I learned that early at my house. And I'm glad that I did.

When I was in college, I went to a friend's wedding. At the reception I was introduced to his aunt. And as soon as she heard my name she started laughing.

"Excuse me for laughing, but is your dad Jim Farrar?"

"Yes, that's my dad."

"I'm sorry for laughing, Steve, but the last time I saw you was about fifteen years ago. You were sitting in the front row at church. You were probably five or six years old. And in the middle of the pastor's invitation at the end of the service, you pulled a yo-yo out of your pocket and started to practice. I will never forget your father reaching over two pews and discreetly picking you up by the back of your pants and pulling you back to where he and your mother were sitting. His hand just about covered your entire back and he did it so effortlessly and quietly that hardly anyone knew what happened!"

I didn't remember that incident. But it certainly explained to me why every time I got near a yo-yo, I would begin to shake uncontrollably (just kidding). In our family, you didn't mess around when you went to church. You respected what was happening in the house of the Lord.

BARBARIAN PRIESTS

It's too bad Eli didn't teach his boys the same thing. You may remember that Eli was a priest of Israel. Eli served the Lord for forty years. And during some of those years he mentored the great prophet Samuel. Eli lived in a day much like today. It was the time of the judges, possibly one of the most evil periods of Israelite history. The nation had abandoned

Moses' teaching of Deuteronomy 6, and every man did what was right in his own eyes.

Eli had two sons, Hophni and Phinehas, who grew up to become priests like their father. But there was a problem with his sons. They were described in 1 Samuel 2:12 as "worthless men; they did not know the LORD." The more exact translation of "worthless men" is "sons of Belial," which in a nutshell means that they were barbarians. Hophni and Phinehas were in positions of spiritual leadership in Israel, but they did not know the Lord.

In 1 Samuel 2, several charges were leveled against these two sons. First, they broke the law in three different ways when they made their priestly offerings before the Lord. But in addition, they were practicing immorality.

> Now Eli was very old; and he heard all that his sons were doing to all Israel, and how they lay with the women who served at the doorway of the tent of meeting.
>
> And he said to them, "Why do you do such things, the evil things that I hear from all these people? No, my sons; for the report is not good which I hear the LORD's people circulating. If one man sins against another, God will mediate for him; but if a man sins against the LORD, who can intercede for him?" But they would not listen to the voice of their father, for the LORD desired to put them to death. (vv. 22–25)

Obviously, these sons had never learned the "fear of the Lord." They had no respect for the Lord or the sacrifices that were to be made to Him. And because of their refusal to fear the Lord, God killed them.

> And the LORD said to Samuel, "Behold, I am about to do a thing in Israel at which both ears of everyone who hears it will tingle. In that day I will carry out against Eli

all that I have spoken concerning his house, from beginning to end. For I have told him that I am about to judge his house forever for the iniquity which he knew, because his sons brought a curse on themselves *and he did not rebuke them.*" (1 Sam. 3:11–13, emphasis added)

I'm sure that Eli not only loved the Lord, but he loved his sons. No doubt he loved them from the moment he first held them. But Eli had missed the boat when it came to enforcing the fifth commandment in his home: "Honor your father and your mother, that your days may be prolonged in the land which the LORD your God gives you" (Ex. 20:12).

Perhaps Eli had wanted to avoid confrontation with his sons. Perhaps his own fear of failure or rejection kept him from teaching them the fear of the Lord. Perhaps they were both "strong-willed," rather than compliant. And it was simply easier just to let them have their way. We don't know all that happened in their years of growing up. But what we do know is that Eli failed his sons. He failed to love them with the true love of a father because he did not rebuke them.

My son, do not regard lightly the discipline of the LORD,
Nor faint when you are reproved by Him;
For those whom the LORD loves He disciplines. (Heb. 12:5)

Our perfect heavenly Father loves us. And because He loves us, He disciplines us. The most loving thing that a father can do for his child is to discipline his child.

And so Eli stood by and watched his sons as they lived scandalous lives. When he finally did rebuke them, it was too late. His sons were not listening. The greatest tragedy for this father was that eventually, his failure to discipline his sons cost them their lives.

Do you want your children to turn out like Eli's sons? Obviously not. You want your children to learn the fear of the

Lord. So they had better develop a healthy fear of you. And they had better learn it early on. Not a "terror" of you. Just a healthy fear that you mean what you say, and that it would be a wise move on their part to cooperate. That perception will save them from a lot of grief and heartache down the road.

A LITERAL FEAR

In my study on the fear of the Lord, I came across a very good article by a conservative scholar. He covered all of the Scriptures that mentioned the fear of the Lord, and he drew some excellent observations. But then he said something that absolutely floored me. He wrote that "the fear of the Lord is not a literal fear." Oh, really?

Try telling that to Hophni and Phinehas. Or how about Nadab and Abihu. Remember those two guys? They were the two sons of Aaron who offered strange fire to the Lord. And they, too, were killed (Lev. 10). Or how about Ananias and Sapphira in Acts 5? They lied to the Holy Spirit and were struck dead by God. And what was the response of the other people in the church? Acts 5:11 says, "And great fear came upon the whole church, and upon all who heard of these things." I think that's what you would call a literal fear.

Can you imagine two adults lying to the Holy Spirit? That's what happened in the early church. Lying to the Holy Spirit is a very, very, serious matter. But it wasn't serious to Ananias and Sapphira. They had become such habitual liars that they lied before a holy God without blinking an eyelid. And they were struck dead. It's too bad they didn't have fathers who disciplined them when they lied as children. That discipline could have saved their lives.

It's unfortunate that Hollywood totally misses the value of disciplining children and holding them to a standard.

Consistently the film industry paints fathers in one of two ways. There is the Saddam Hussein father, a fundamentalist weirdo who enjoys punishing his children and doesn't contain a human bone in his body. Or there is the foolish Al Bundy father of *Married with Children,* who is totally clueless and, I might add, totally depraved. But the biblical father is neither. He is a balanced, loving father, full of mercy and grace. He also knows when to discipline. The fear of that kind of father is more than healthy. It preserves a nation.

I saw a cartoon the other day that hit the nail on the head. A five-year-old boy has been sitting on the couch watching TV when his mother comes into the room. She reaches to turn the set off, saying, "A new study says TV desensitizes children by not showing the consequences of violence, so let's turn it off." Behind her back, her five-year-old holds up a pistol and says to his mother, "Back away. Very slowly."

ISN'T SPANKING ABUSE?

Another cartoon in the *Wall Street Journal* caught my attention as well. A father and mother are seated across the desk from the school counselor. The counselor says, "Mr. and Mrs. Nelson, your son is vicious, mean-spirited, disloyal, and has a tendency to spread rumors. I suggest a career in journalism."

I know some wonderful Christian people who are in the media. But those who hold biblical values are few and far between in the media. Newspapers, magazines, and "special reports" on network shows consistently equate spanking with abuse. In fact, it has become so much the prevailing consensus that laws have even been passed in some parts of the country forbidding parents to spank their children. All the while, escalating crime among our youth threatens to be our undoing.

These foolish child "experts" who portray spanking as abusive have never read Proverbs, the book of wisdom. Spanking, says Proverbs, is not abuse. It is, rather, wise fathering.

> *He who spares his rod hates his son,*
> *But he who loves him disciplines him promptly.*
> (Prov. 13:24 NKJV)

> **All discipline for the moment seems not to be joyful, but sorrowful; yet to those who have been trained by it, afterwards it yields the peaceful fruit of righteousness.**
> (Heb. 12:11)

Biblical spanking does not abuse children. It trains and builds children. The idea that child-rearing should be pain-free is not only foolish, it is impossible. Every loving parent inflicts a necessary degree of pain on their children. In fact, the government requires every parent to inflict pain. No, I'm not talking about spanking. I'm talking about inoculations.

SOUL INOCULATIONS

How many parents do you know who wouldn't think of not inoculating their children? Their children may scream, and even faint (as one of ours did), but no loving parent is going to let that stop him. Why do we let someone poke our children with needles? Because we know that the inoculation will save them from something far more serious down the road. None of us want our children to get polio or diphtheria. If we could inoculate them for every deadly disease, we would. Why? Because we love them.

Discipline is the inoculation of our little children's souls. The pain of discipline early on can prevent overwhelming pain and discomfort down the road. When a parent spanks his child, is he telling the child to hit other children? Far from it. He is telling the child *not* to hit. He is telling the child that he cares about him enough that he is willing to stop him from destructive behavior. And children intuitively understand this.

ANY EXCESS IS HARMFUL

The fact is that "any disciplinary measure, physical, verbal or emotional, if carried to an extreme, can harm a child."[10] You could ground a teenager for a year . . . that's probably excessive. You could verbally berate and tear down a young child for several days after a disobedient act . . . that's excessive. You could send a child to his room and not let him come out for several weeks . . . that, too, is excessive. Any of those excessive acts are extreme. But an appropriate spanking, administered by a loving father who is in control of his emotions, on the bottom of a child who was warned in advance of the consequences of disobedience, is not abuse. It is an act of love.

Sometimes a child will ask a father about the difference between hitting and spanking. I heard of one little boy who asked his dad why he wasn't supposed to hit kids at school but it was all right for his father to spank him. Spanking and hitting are not the same thing. Fathers who hit their children abuse their children. There is a big difference between a biblical spanking and physical abuse.

The Family Research Council put together this helpful chart that demonstrates the differences between spanking and abuse:[11]

	Spanking	**Physical Abuse**
Act	Spanking: One or two spanks to the buttocks repeatedly	Beating: To strike (Also kick, punch, choke)
Intent	Training: To correct problem behavior	Violence: Physical force intended to injure or abuse
Attitude	With love and concern	With anger and malice
Effects	Behavioral correction	Emotional and physical injury

God is not abusive to His children. And the instructions that He gives to fathers in regard to the disciplining of their children are not abusive or excessive. Let's take a quick glimpse at some of the instructions that are recorded in the book of Proverbs on discipline.

By the way, don't be put off by the word *rod* that we find in the book of Proverbs. A biblical "rod" is not a steel rein-forcement rod with nails welded onto it. It is true that the Hebrew word for rod can mean a club or even the shaft of a spear.[12] But according to noted Hebrew scholar Dr. Bruce Waltke, it does not have that meaning in the book of Proverbs. "In Proverbs, the word *rod* is used as the *symbol* of disci-pline" (emphasis added).[13] "Rod" is found eight times in Proverbs, and in each case it means or has reference to the application of discipline.[14]

"Rod" refers to an instrument of discipline like a switch (which my mom preferred), a yardstick (which she preferred when I got big enough to laugh at the switch), a ruler (which my third-grade teacher, Mrs. Lemert, preferred), a Ping-Pong paddle (which I preferred because of the two layers of rubber on each side that, unbeknownst to my parents, took the sting out of it), or that great faithful standby, the good, old Amer-ican leather belt (which my dad preferred and used with great skill, dexterity, and phenomenal hand-eye coordination). I'm grateful that he loved me enough to teach me the fear of the Lord. And it all began with a fear of the belt.

John Owen was right when he said, "We ought as much to pray for a blessing on our daily rod as upon our daily bread."

Note the wisdom and common sense of Proverbs:

- "A wise son makes a father glad, / But a foolish man despises his mother." (15:20)
- "A foolish son is a grief to his father, / And bitterness to her who bore him." (17:25)
- "A foolish son is destruction to his father." (19:13)
- "Discipline your son while there is hope, / And do not desire his death." (19:18)
- "Foolishness is bound up in the heart of a child; / The rod of discipline will remove it far from him." (22:15)
- "Do not hold back discipline from the child, / Although you beat him with the rod [swat him with a switch, etc.], he will not die. / You shall beat him with the rod, / And deliver his soul from Sheol." (23:13–14)
- "The rod and reproof give wisdom, / But a child who gets his own way brings shame to his mother." (29:15)
- "Correct your son, and he will give you comfort; / He will also delight your soul." (29:17)

PRINCIPLES OF DISCIPLINE

An entire book could be written on child discipline. But I'm just doing one chapter on it, and I am quickly running out of pages. So in summary form, let me offer ten principles of disciplining children.

1. Start Early in Disciplining Your Child

How early? Dr. James Dobson suggests that mild spankings can begin between fifteen and eighteen months. From my personal experience, I think he is right on the money. Note the emphasis on "mild." You obviously are going to handle an eighteen-month-old toddler differently from an eight-year-old.

My daughter, Rachel, is now finishing her senior year of high school. We are very grateful to have a daughter of Rachel's caliber. She teaches a freshman girl's Bible study of about twenty-five girls that meets at our house weekly. She is a varsity cheerleader and a leader at school. She is deeply committed to the Lord and to serving Him. So we are very fortunate and very grateful. But she was a strong-willed little sucker.

It was right around the age of fifteen or sixteen months that Rachel's strong will kicked into full gear. Mary and I began to find ourselves faced with the strong will of this little baby girl on a daily basis. Being a natural-born leader, she was highly motivated to be in charge of our family at certain key times. And, of course, that wasn't going to work.

I have vivid memories of playing Ping-Pong in my garage one particular evening. I was playing with my good friend John Brandon. Rachel was in her little portable chair with wheels, scooting around the garage. After a few minutes, she got very upset that I wasn't focused on her. She let me know in her precocious vocabulary that she wanted me to stop and play with her, "right now!" I stopped and explained to her that I would be done in a few minutes, and then I would play with her. Until then, she had her scooter and her toys. You need to know that this little girl was anything but deprived of my attention. It was actually a rare thing for me to play a game of Ping-Pong.

A few seconds later, she started to throw a fit. Good fathers do not allow their children to start the habit of throwing fits. So I walked over to her and took her little hand and gave her a little swat with my hand. She was too small at that point to use another object. (As my kids got older, I tended not to use my hand.) It was actually more of a flick than a swat. But it got her attention. And, like a riled-up little bee, it made her even more mad.

To show me her anger, she began to yell a little louder with more defiance. So I flicked her hand again, with just a little bit more behind it than the first time. That really got her mad. Then she started a five-alarm defiant scream. And may I underscore the term *defiant*.

Suddenly, I realized that I was in a classic, eye-to-eye, will-to-will confrontation with the defiant will of this beautiful little girl. And I could not allow her to get the upper hand. I forgot about John, and I forgot about winning the Ping-Pong match. John had enough sense to know what was going on, and he sort of faded away out of sight. I had a far more important battle on my hands. Perhaps I would lose to John in Ping-Pong, but I was not going to lose to Rachel. There was simply too much riding on it.

At this point, I lifted her up out of her little chair, put her in my lap, and once again said, "No, Rachel!" This time there was more zip in the flick, just enough to sting her little hand. And that was all it took.

Suddenly, the defiance was gone. It was gone from her attitude and it was absent from her crying. Do you know what I mean when I say that? Her crying immediately changed gears from a defiant, rebellious, self-centered crying to a crying of submission and sorrow. And I held her and told her how much I loved her. I remember her convulsive little sobs of sorrow. Then, with tears running down her cheeks, she said, "I'm sorry, Daddy." And I knew that she really was.

I remember that evening just like it was yesterday. And one of the reasons that I remember is because, right in the middle of it, I had a very clear sense in the back of my mind that this was a battle that was going to have implications for my daughter for years to come. There was something about that episode in the garage that summer evening that I knew was going to have long-term implications for the quality of Rachel's life.

That was not the last battle with Rachel's strong will. Some battles in the next few years were tougher than others. But each one was a life-and-death matter. Rachel's development as a person, her relationship with Christ, her place and role in our family, and even her life one day as a wife and mother— these were always hanging in the balance.

As her father, I had to love her enough to deal with her until her hard spirit broke and became soft. And for you dads who have a strong-willed child, I have good news for you. The day came when Rachel yielded her strong will to Christ. And a strong will placed in the hand of God is a wonderful thing. Her spiritual fortitude and commitment have made all of those tough battles worth it all.

Hard spirits and wills don't yield to Christ. And so many times, the earthly reason that they don't is that they were never trained early to yield to loving authority.

2. Use Discipline for Training, Not Humiliation or Venting of Anger

Never discipline out of anger. Because if you do, you will have accomplished nothing but destruction. Anger is natural, especially when your child is defiant and disobedient. But you are the adult here. You need to grab hold of your anger, and put yourself under the control of Christ. When we discipline out of anger, we do stupid things and we say stupid things.

What would happen if God simply vented His anger upon us? We probably would not be having this conversation today. Neither should you vent your anger upon your children. For you will surely destroy them. God disciplines us for training. And that is our goal. We are Christian fathers, and our purpose in discipline is to *train our children in righteousness.* "He disciplines us for our good, that we may share His holiness. All discipline for the moment seems not to be joyful, but sorrowful; yet to those who have been trained by it, afterwards it yields the peaceful fruit of righteousness" (Heb. 12:10–11).

A parent who is always losing it at home, or who is constantly yelling at and slapping his child in public, has accomplished only one thing. He has succeeded in planting a bitter spirit within his child. And a child who is bitter toward his dad will tend to become bitter toward God.

So, discipline with forethought, with respect, and with the intent to train.

And one more thing. Discipline in private, not in public.

Discipline is between you and your child. It is not a public trial. But what if your child throws a fit in the grocery store? And he's eighteen years old? (Just kidding, although some of you aren't laughing!) If a child throws a fit in the grocery store, pick him up, leave the cart right where it is, and take him out of the store. Depending on the circumstances, either discipline him in the car or drive directly home and discipline him there. Now if you live thirty miles from the grocery store that is not going to work. A young child will forget what he did wrong by the time you get home. But I think you get my drift.

I had a situation happen with one of my sons last month. I asked him to get something out of the car for me. Instead of doing it, he gave me a couple of reasons why he didn't want to do it. He was sort of half kidding and making a joke. But I didn't think it was funny. He knew immediately by the tone of my voice that I *wasn't* kidding. And so he quickly made his way to the car. By the way, this took place in the office of a good friend, who was watching the exchange. Was that the place to discipline? No, it wasn't. But when we left my friend's office we dealt with the situation immediately.

3. Deal Swiftly with Disrespect

We have a virtual epidemic of disrespectful children. The film industry loves to feature these modern-day foulmouthed and smart-alecky kids. But disrespect goes hand in hand with lack of fear. They are like two sides of the same coin.

Disrespect comes in all kinds of forms. It can be seen in body language, reluctance to obey, facial expressions, and of course, words. But in whatever form it comes, we cannot allow it in our homes. Disrespect is lethal. We have to deal with it swiftly and severely, the same way that you would if your child were pointing a loaded gun at you.

God commanded children to honor, or respect, their fathers *and mothers*. And fathers, your wives are depending on you for this one. A woman finds herself at a distinct disadvantage when she is faced with a six-foot-two, 175-pound male child. One of your primary roles is to make sure he shows respect toward his mother. If you want to ruin your child's life, allow him to talk disrespectfully to your wife. Sons who disrespect their mothers grow up to be lousy husbands. And daughters who disrespect their mothers grow up to be rebellious and miserable.

Absolutely insist on respect.

4. Discipline Rebellion and Defiance, Not Childish Mistakes

If you are a new father, you should know about the "law of juice." What is the "law of juice"? It is a natural law that Mary and I discovered after raising three young children. The law is simply this. If you go to the grocery store to buy a gallon of apple juice, buy two gallons. In other words, if you need one gallon, always buy two. Because the "law of juice" dictates that precisely half the juice that a father provides for his family will be spilled at each meal. That's the "law of juice."

When a child spills juice reaching for the ketchup, is that rebellion? Is that defiance of a parent? No, it's being a kid. Kids are supposed to spill juice. That's what they are good at. So don't discipline kids for being kids. Cut them some slack. Give them plenty of grace and mercy. That's what God does for you, Dad. So double your juice budget and chill out. And discipline the stuff that really matters.

5. Communicate the Rule Clearly, and Enforce It the First Time

"If I have to tell you one more time." Why would you do that? Discipline the first time. Then you won't have to tell them one more time.

But make certain that you have made the rules clear. Don't ask your child to do something that you haven't taken the time to show him or explain.

6. Make Sure Your Child Understands Why He Is Being Disciplined

I remember a situation several years ago with Josh when I spanked him and he was absolutely crushed. He didn't understand what he had done wrong. And in that situation I was wrong. I had broken my own rule. It is best before disciplining a child to simply say, "Son, the reason that I'm going to discipline you is this. Do you understand why I'm going to discipline you?"

By the way, this isn't a negotiation period. You simply are making sure that the child understands. If he doesn't understand what he did wrong, training cannot take place.

7. Don't Be Afraid to Make Midcourse Corrections, or to Admit When You Have Been Wrong

Sometimes dads have to remind everyone of the basic principles. Sometimes you sense that the kids are drifting or that you have drifted in your disciplining. If that happens, and it has happened to me, then simply call a family meeting. "Kids, I have realized that in the last few weeks I have not been a good father. I have allowed some things to pass that I should have dealt with. I have been wrong in allowing that to happen. I apologize and I ask your forgiveness. I love you all too much to let that continue. So as of now, we are going back to our basic principles. When they are violated, they will be dealt with the first time. I wanted everyone to know that we are going to correct the drift and we are going to get back on course. Does everyone understand?" And then do it.

8. Husbands and Wives Must Present a United Front to the Children

You may not agree with the action that your wife has taken. But back her up. Save your disagreement to discuss when it's just the two of you. Don't let your kids divide and conquer. Be united in your discipline. Back each other. You will not always agree with your spouse's actions. But take care of those things in private.

9. Always Discipline with Your Child's Personality in Mind

The strong-willed child needs a different approach from that needed for the compliant child. The child who is a perfectionist needs a different approach from the one who flies with the wind. We have to get to our kids, guys, and then treat them each as unique creatures in our discipline. Learn what motivates and demotivates each of your children. And you will discover that your discipline is far more effective.

10. Make Sure the Punishment Fits the Crime

The idea is simply this. Don't ground your child for a year for flunking an exam. Look at the "infraction" and determine what it is that you want your child to learn. Do you want him to learn to share his toys? Then put the toy that he can't seem to share away for a while. Is she talking back on a quite regular basis? Perhaps a little dab of soft soap in the mouth next time will bring it to an end.

Discipline requires a tremendous amount of energy and thought. But the rewards are worth it a hundred times over.

These are some very basic principles. And that's what we have done; we have covered the very basics. What about teenagers? When do you stop spanking? There are hundreds of legitimate questions on this issue of discipline. That's why I want to recommend two excellent biblical treatments of the subject by Dr. James Dobson. If you haven't read *Dare to Discipline,* you have missed a gold mine. And I would also highly recommend Dr. Dobson's *The Strong-Willed Child.*

If you are thinking that you don't need to read *The Strong-Willed Child* because you only have one child and he isn't strong-willed, then you definitely need to read *The Strong-Willed Child*. Because the next child you have will be strong-willed. That's kind of how God does things. And it's how He keeps fathers who think they've got it together humble. He gives them a strong-willed child. And you quickly realize that the only way you are going to keep that child from becoming a barbarian is by the wisdom and grace that come only from the heavenly Father.

In the next five to ten years, your home is headed for either anarchy or revival. So love your kids, discipline your kids, and enjoy the revival.

—7—

BENT BY GOD

"Consider the work of God;
For who is able to straighten what He
has bent?"

—Ecclesiastes 7:13

In the eighteen years that I have been a father, we have had one dog, one cat, one rabbit, two snakes, several turtles, five or six frogs, and four hermit crabs (whatever those are).

But that's not all. At our house we also have a lion, an otter, a beaver, and a golden retriever. You should know that the lion, the otter, and the beaver are not pets. They are my children. And the golden retriever is my wife. For some reason I'm sensing that I'd better explain this. Quickly.

If you have ever heard either Gary Smalley or John Trent speak at one of their conferences, then you immediately recognized what I meant by the lion, the otter, the beaver, and the golden retriever. Each of those animals stands for a basic type of human personality.

PERSONALITY TYPES

These four types of personalities have been understood for centuries. But Gary and John came up with a very creative way of explaining how each of these personalities functions.

Each of your children falls into one of these four basic categories. You might say, "Wait a minute, you're putting my kids in a box." Not at all. Each child is absolutely unique. You know that and so do I. That's why each person is actually a combination of the different traits. It's possible to have a child who is 60 percent lion, 20 percent otter, 10 percent beaver, and 10 percent golden retriever.

Let me give you the description of each type and then you can begin to see from Scripture why it is so important to understand how God designed your child.

The Lion

The lion is a leader. I remember years ago being at the San Francisco zoo when they were feeding the lions. I have never in my life heard such a hair-raising sound as the roar of twenty or so lions.

Here are some of the strengths of the lion: assertive, determined, diligent, courageous, decisive, goal-oriented, persevering, direct, straightforward, purposeful, confident.

Here are some of the weaknesses that lions can have: insensitive, domineering, headstrong, one-track mind, never slow down, stubborn, overly competitive, tactless, disrespectful, self-sufficient, and cocky.

The Otter

If you ever get a chance to visit the Monterey Aquarium in California, do it. It is absolutely world-class. And the otter exhibition is worth its weight in gold. The key word in the life of an otter is *fun*.

The otter has some great strengths: people-person, good communicator, encourager, expressive, dramatic, humorous, imaginative, enthusiastic, persuasive, optimistic, positive, spontaneous, and flexible.

And of course, some weaknesses: They are more prone to give in to peer pressure, they tend to be overly concerned about what others think of them. They can talk too much and interrupt. They can be very smooth talkers but poor listeners, and they have a tendency to exaggerate, clown around too much, and daydream. They are often disorganized and impulsive.

The Beaver

There's a creek a few miles from our house that has been dammed up by some beavers. As many times as I've been at the creek, I've yet to see a beaver. But it's impossible to miss their work. Beavers are the builders and engineers.

They have some important strengths: analytical, curious, cautious, conscientious, objective, discerning, serious-minded, prepared, self-controlled, industrous, and they have high standards of work.

Some related weaknesses are: overly critical, cynical, ask too many questions, unsociable, skeptical, tend to worry, and lean toward perfectionism. At times they can be unfeeling and you may find it hard to follow their logic. They can take too much time to complete assignments, be too demanding or exacting of themselves and others, and at times, nitpicky.

The Golden Retriever

A dog is man's best friend and among all dogs you will find no more loyal friend than a golden retriever. People who have golden retriever traits will show the following strengths: They are accepting, content, helpful, cooperative, softhearted, compassionate, submissive, obedient, good listeners, steady, modest, and reliable.

As a result, they usually display some of the following weaknesses: lack conviction, too lenient, lazy, unmotivated, overly accommodating, wishy-washy. They at times can be easily influenced, yet it is not unusual for them to resist change. They often discount their own abilities, resist compliments, and can be taken advantage of.

This is all very interesting, but what's the point? The point is this. Each of your kids is different. They have different strengths and they have different weaknesses. They have been custom-designed by God. And it's your job to help them discover how they have been wired.

Chuck Swindoll realizes how critical this issue is:

> If parents were to ask me, "What is the greatest gift we could give our child?" . . . my counsel to you would be, give your child the time it takes to find out how he or she is put together. Help your child know who he or she is. Help them know themselves so that they learn to love and accept themselves as they are. Then, as they move into a society that seems so committed to pounding them into another shape, they will remain true to themselves, secure in their independent walk with God.[1]

Back in the 1940s Notre Dame had a center by the name of Frank Syzmanski. Syzmanski was called to be a witness for a lawsuit that was filed against the athletic department.

The judge asked him, "Are you the starting center on the Notre Dame football team?"

"Yes I am, Your Honor," replied Syzmanski.

"How good of a center are you?" asked the judge.

Syzmanski hesitated for a minute and said, "Your Honor, I am the finest center in the history of Notre Dame football."

The Notre Dame football coach, Joe Leahy, was sitting in the courtroom. He was stunned by Syzmanski's announcement since he had always been such a quiet and unassuming player. During a recess, Leahy asked him about his statement.

Syzmanski blushed and said, "I'm sorry, Coach. But I was under oath and I had to tell the truth."

Whether anyone else believed it or not, deep down inside, Frank Syzmanski believed that he had a unique strength. In his heart he didn't doubt it for a minute. There was no confusion inside this quiet young man about who he was or what he could do.

Your children need to develop that same quiet confidence in who they are and in how God has put them together. And it's your job as a father to help them make the discovery.

STRENGTHS AND BENTS

When I was in school I hated math. In fact, *hate* is not quite a strong enough word. I loathed math. I despised math. Yea, verily, I even despaired of math.

But I loved to read. And I loved to write. I just seemed to be "bent" that way.

When you were in school, what classes did you really enjoy? What classes did you hate? What class interested you so much that you never watched the clock? Were you "bent" toward math? Or maybe you were "bent" toward chemistry.

I have a good friend who only enjoyed shop classes. He didn't do too well in anything else. But he had a real strength in shop classes. Any kind of shop classes. Metal shop, wood shop, auto shop—this guy was incredible. He was just "bent" toward shop. His parents were kind of worried about him because he didn't do real well academically. Today he owns a chain of automobile repair shops. And he does better financially than 95 percent of the kids who outdid him in academics.

Usually, in the same family, there will be one child who is gifted in math and one who isn't. The one who isn't gifted in math may be off the charts when it comes to reading comprehension. But his sister, who is so good at math, struggles to keep up with her brother in reading. Same father; different kids. Different bents; different strengths.

In our society, children who do well in school and get high scores on the SAT are considered to be "smart." The kids who just barely get along in school aren't usually thought of as "smart." Nothing could be farther from the truth.

Thomas Armstrong has written a book called *Seven Kinds of Smart*.[2] Armstrong demonstrates that there are at least seven different types of intelligence and the American education system is designed to recognize only two of the seven types. I'm using Armstrong's research but I'm changing his labels to make them a little more clear. Here are the seven kinds of intelligence and a few possible professions that seem to go along with them:

1. The intelligence of words—writers, speakers, etc.
2. The intelligence of numbers—engineers, computer programmers, accountants, etc.
3. The intelligence of pictures and images—architects, photographers, artists, etc.
4. The intelligence of music—singers, musicians, composers
5. The intelligence of the physical body—athletes, craftsmen, surgeons
6. The intelligence of understanding people—counselors, networkers, camp directors
7. The intelligence of introspection and thinking—philosophers, theologians

Just about everyone is intelligent. We are just intelligent in different areas. And each human being comes out of the womb "bent" toward at least one, and in most cases, more than one of the different kinds of "smart."

Who did the bending? God did. Do I have any biblical basis to say that fathers are responsible for teaching their children to understand and discover the strengths that God has built into them? Actually, I don't.

Just kidding. I wanted to see if you were still with me. I believe that there is a very strong case biblically that fathers are to teach their children to discover and realize their God-given strengths. Or, to put it another way, fathers are responsible to teach their children about their God-given "bents." There is a very familiar verse that I have in mind. And it's Proverbs 22:6.

> *Train up a child in the way he should go,*
> *And when he is old he will not depart from it.* (NKJV)

This verse has generally been understood to mean that if you raise a child in a Christian home and make sure that he learns the Bible in Sunday school, and at some point in his youth he rebels and turns away from God, then one day he will eventually return to God.

That's not what that verse means. It's not even close.

Twenty years ago, Chuck Swindoll wrote a book that he titled *You and Your Child.* In my opinion, it's the single best volume on raising children from a biblical perspective that I have ever read (it's still in print and wise fathers will get their hands on a copy). Chuck had a section where he explained Proverbs 22:6 in great detail. And his explanation blew me away. It was different from the typical understanding of this verse. But as usual, Chuck had done his homework. He offered this expanded translation of Proverbs 22:6 to really get the punch of what Solomon was saying: "Adapt the training of your child so that *it is in keeping with his God-given characteristics and tendencies;* when he comes to maturity, he will not depart from the training that he has received."[3]

The Amplified Bible translates Proverbs 22:6 with the same sense: "Train up a child in the way he should go [*and in keeping with his individual gift or bent*], and when he is old he will not depart from it" (emphasis added).

Children are born with bents. And those bents are from God. Some kids are bent toward art. Some kids are bent toward numbers. Some kids are bent toward speech. Some kids are bent toward mechanics. Some kids are bent toward other people. Some kids are bent toward nurturing. Some kids are bent toward being quiet and thoughtful. Some kids are bent toward large groups. Some kids are bent toward small groups.

Again, those bents have been built into your child by God. And it is the father's responsibility to understand those bents and help his child to understand and appreciate how he or she is bent.

Chuck put it this way:

> In every child God places in our arms, there is a bent, a set of characteristics already established. The bent is fixed and determined before he is given over to our care. The child is not, in fact, a pliable piece of clay. He has been set; he has been bent. And the parents who want to train this child correctly will discover that bent![4]

It would have been sad if

- Billy Graham ran a gas station in North Carolina.
- Luciano Pavarotti sold software in Rome.
- Albert Einstein was a cook at Princeton.
- Michael Jordan was an attorney in Chicago.
- Henry Ford repaired Maytags in Detroit.
- Norman Schwarzkopf was a general contractor in Tampa.

God bends every person He creates in a unique way so that they can function and play the part in His universe that He has ordained. As Proverbs 22:29 puts it:

Do you see a man skilled in his work?
He will stand before kings.

God bends a child a certain way for a reason. God gives a child certain gifts for a reason. God gives unique gifts to children for a reason. And it is the responsibility of the Christian father to help his child understand the way that God has bent him.

Two Christian men, Ralph Mattson and Arthur Miller, have done some great thinking about "bents."

> There are thousands of young people who are accused of not having direction in their lives, *and most of them want direction but do not know how to find it*. There are tens of thousands of adults who want some sense of purpose in their workday lives, but who have little knowledge of how to go about getting it. There are hundreds of thousands of people who spend their lives as if they were adrift—trapped in their circumstances. There are millions of housewives, students, salesmen, bosses, waitresses, executives, ministers, and auto mechanics who do not fit the lives they lead.
>
> Most people are uncertain about the rightness and usefulness of their lives. They are looking for signposts that will give them purpose and direction.[5]

Good fathers help their children to understand and appreciate the strengths that God has placed within them. The reason that so many people are clueless about who they are is that they didn't have fathers who plugged into them. And now as adults, they are deeply struggling.

When I say teach a child about his strengths, what I really mean is that you *encourage* him in his strengths. You give him feedback. You let him know that God has given him strengths. You affirm those strengths. You let him know that you think that God has something special in mind for him to do with those strengths.

Charlie Hedges lays out some great insight:

> I could never be a concert pianist or a professional basketball player or a surgeon or a dentist. I don't have the physical talents to perform those highly skilled tasks. Neither could I be a therapist who specializes in long-term care . . . I don't have the talents or patience to work with slow and minimal change. I'm "built" to do other things, and when I'm doing those things, I receive much more satisfaction from my efforts.
>
> Many people visit career counseling offices because they attained success in fields that are outside their natural talents. They learned to excel, but not enjoy. . . .
>
> My job as a parent is *not* to direct my son to a certain career. And yet that is what too many parents do. Do you know why? Because many of us were raised that way. In her career counseling, my wife says that one of the most destructive messages her clients must deal with is the parental message. "You should be a doctor . . . a lawyer . . . a painter . . . a teacher . . ."[6]

Miller and Mattson agree:

> Probably like you, we had been brought up with the idea that we could be anything we wanted. Being Americans, we thought from our earliest years that all options were open to us if we were willing to work hard enough. We could become doctors or potters or lawyers or teachers or carpenters or actors or artists or plumbers—whatever we wanted. All we had to have was some talent to develop. In some cases, if

we were willing to practice hard enough, we might even develop the talents we otherwise did not possess.

Then we encountered evidence that said otherwise. We discovered that people could not become anything they wanted. They could only become what was in harmony with who they were designed to be . . . we discovered that a pattern of voluntary behavior emerged early in the life of every person we evaluated. More than that, we could see that the pattern remained consistent throughout the individual's life. . . . In over three thousand cases, there was not one exception. . . . People begin with a specific design that remains consistent through life and cannot be changed.[7]

What these guys are talking about is bents. The bents that God puts into every child. God builds and bends every child with particular strengths. Parents are constantly telling their children they can be whatever they want to be. That's really not right.

Michael Green tells the story of a mother who returned home from attending a national convention of feminists. She was greeted by her five-year-old daughter, who said, "While you were gone, Mommy, I decided what I want to be when I grow up."

"Oh, that's wonderful," replied the mother, thrilled that her daughter was already thinking of pursuing a meaningful career outside the home. "What do you want to be?"

"I want to be a nurse" said the little girl.

The mother could barely hide her disappointment.

"You don't have to settle for being a nurse, honey. You can be an airline pilot, or the head of a large corporation, or the president of the United States. You can be anything you want."

The little girl replied, "I can be *anything* I want?"

"Of course you can, sweetheart!"

The little girl thought for a moment and said, "I'll be a horse."

How did Miller and Mattson put it? They discovered that people could only become what was in harmony with who they were designed to be. And the wise father will take that into consideration when encouraging his child.

- When a child understands his strengths he will be fulfilled.
- When a child is encouraged in his strengths he will be fulfilled.
- When a child grows up and works in his area of strength he will be fulfilled because he is using the strengths that God has put within him.
- When a person is working in his area of strength, others will benefit. When a person works in his area of strength, he will have a happier family and a happier life because he is doing what God has gifted him to do.

That's why it's very important that you help your children understand how God has wired them.

A few years ago, I was with my family during spring break in a rustic lodge high in the Cascade Mountains of Oregon. I spent a couple of days with my editor putting the finishing touches on a book and then we were going to spend some time using a friend's snowmobiles and maybe even going skiing. But instead of snow, we got rain. It rained the first day and it rained the second day.

We were all pretty disappointed and looking for some other things to do. That afternoon we went into town to look around. I walked into a bookstore and found a nugget. That night after dinner, as we were all sitting around the fire, I said, "I found a story this afternoon in the bookstore that I would like to read to you."

Now my three kids at this point were twelve, ten, and seven. And they didn't want to hear the story. They all indicated to me that they had outgrown my reading them bedtime stories.

"Well, this isn't a bedtime story and you don't have to go to bed when it's over. It's just a pretty good story."

When they heard they didn't have to go to bed they were all willing to hear the story. And here it is. Read this slowly and thoughtfully. You may want to use it later with your kids.

Imagine there is a meadow. In that meadow there is a duck, a fish, an eagle, an owl, a squirrel, and a rabbit. They decide they want to have a school so they can be smart, just like people.

With the help of some grown up animals, they come up with a curriculum they believe will make a well-rounded animal:

> *running,*
> *swimming,*
> *tree climbing,*
> *jumping,*
> *and flying.*

On the first day of school, little br'er rabbit combed his ears and went hopping off to running class.

There he was a star. He ran to the top of the hill and back as fast as he could, and oh, did it feel good. He said to himself, "I can't believe it. At school, I get to do what I do best."

The instructor said: "Rabbit, you really have talent for running. You have great muscles in your rear legs. With some training, you will get more out of every hop."

The rabbit said, "I love school. I get to do what I like to do and get to learn to do it better."

The next class was swimming. When the rabbit smelled the chlorine, he said, "Wait, wait! Rabbits don't like to swim."

The instructor said, "Well, you may not like it now, but five years from now you'll know it was a good thing for you."

In the tree-climbing class, a tree trunk was set at a 30-degree angle so all the animals had a chance to succeed. The little rabbit tried so hard that he hurt his leg.

In jumping class, the rabbit got along just fine; in flying class, he had a problem. So the teacher gave him a psychological test and discovered he belonged in remedial flying.

In remedial flying class, the rabbit had to practice jumping off a cliff. They told him if he'd just work hard enough, he could succeed.

The next morning, he went on to swimming class. The instructor said, "Today, we jump into the water."

The rabbit panicked. "Wait, wait! I talked to my parents about swimming. They never learned to swim. We don't like to get wet in our family. I'd like to drop this course."

The instructor said, "You can't drop it. The drop-add period is over. At this point you have a choice: Either you jump in or you flunk."

The rabbit jumped in. He panicked! He went down once. He went down twice. Bubbles came up. The instructor saw he was drowning and pulled him out. The other animals had never seen anything quite as funny as this wet rabbit who looked more like a rat without a tail, and so they chirped, and jumped, and barked, and laughed at the rabbit. The rabbit was more humiliated than he had ever been in his life. He wanted desperately to get out of class that day. He was glad when it was over.

He thought that he would head home, that his parents would understand and help him. When he arrived, he said to his parents, "I don't like school. I just want to be free."

"If the rabbits are going to get ahead, you have to get a diploma," replied his parents.

The rabbit said, "I don't want a diploma."

The parents said, "You're going to get a diploma whether you want one or not."

They argued, and finally the parents made the rabbit go to bed. In the morning he headed off to school with a slow hop. Then he remembered that the principal had said that any time he had a problem to remember that the counselor's door was always open.

When he arrived at school, he hopped up in the chair by the counselor and said, "I don't like school."

And the counselor said, "Hmmm, tell me about it."

And the rabbit did.

The counselor said, "Rabbit, I hear you. I hear you saying you don't like school because you don't like swimming. I think I have diagnosed that correctly. Rabbit, I tell you what we'll do. You're doing just fine in running. I don't know why you need to work on running. What you need to do work on is swimming. I'll arrange it so you don't have to go running anymore, and you can have two periods of swimming."

When the rabbit heard that, he threw up.

As the rabbit hopped out of the counselor's office, he looked and saw his old friend, the Wise Old Owl, who cocked his head and said, "Br'er rabbit, life doesn't have to be that way. We could have schools and businesses where people are allowed to concentrate on what they do well."

Br'er rabbit was inspired. He thought when he graduated, he would start a business where the rabbits would do nothing but run, the squirrels could just climb trees, and the fish could just swim. As he disappeared in the meadow, he sighed softly to himself and said, "Oh, what a great place that would be."[8]

I closed the book and looked at my family. Everyone was very still and thoughtful as the fire quietly roared in the background. And then John, who was ten, said, "That would be heaven."

"Why do you think that, John?"

"Because it would be great to be able to do what you're good at and not have to do all the time what you're not good at."

Well, that started a two-hour discussion around the fire as the rain continued to come down outside.

I said, "Here's what we are going to do. We are going to go around the room and talk about what strengths God has given to each of us. Let's start with Rachel, because she is the oldest. And each of us will have a turn to say what we think are Rachel's strengths. We're not going to mention any weaknesses. Just strengths. And then we'll do the same for John and Josh."

That evening was one of the greatest times we have ever had as a family. Every member of our family was affirmed. Every member of our family heard positive things about themselves being expressed by people who loved them the most. And every child went to bed that evening with a greater understanding and appreciation of how God had wired them. Each child is different yet each child is valuable.

Perhaps your family could benefit as we did from an evening like that.

A FATHER NEEDS TO KNOW HIS OWN STRENGTHS FIRST

Do you enjoy what you do for a living? Do you look forward to going to work? Or do you dread going to work? Are you dreaming of retirement and you're twenty-two years old? Or is the thought of retirement a joke for you? Why would you retire when you are having so much fun? Now maybe when you hit sixty-five or seventy you might go in a little later in the morning, or take a few more days off, or work three or four days a week, but you can't imagine not doing what you're doing because you love it so much.

If you love what you're doing, it's because you are using a God-given strength. If you don't love your work, it's because you are not working in an area of strength. You are working in an area of weakness. And God didn't design you to work in your weaknesses. He designed you to use that particular set of strengths and gifts that He gave to you.

Let me clarify. You can work in an area of strength and have a lousy boss. You can work in an area of strength and not be fairly compensated. But your frustrations in those situations are different from those of the guy who is working in a job where he is not strong. At the right time you can get another job and a better boss and a better salary, but if you are working in an area of strength, you are miles ahead of the guy who is working in his weakness with a good boss and a good salary.

One reason that so many men have difficulty helping their children discover their strengths is that as men they don't know their own strengths. It's tough for a father who is unsettled about his own strengths to coach a son or daughter to discover his or her strengths. That's why so many men I talk with are frustrated about the kind of work they do.

My friend Bobb Biehl has done a lot of thinking about work. And he has talked with hundreds of men about their work. And the vast majority of these men were fathers:

> Many leaders I have talked to over the last ten years have concluded that they are very successful in their careers,

but these careers are not necessarily what they want to do for the rest of their lives. They are seeking what I refer to as their life work.[9]

So how does a man find what Bobb refers to as his "life work"? There are a number of characteristics, but here are several that will give you a feel for whether or not you have found your life work. Bobb's personal comments follow each trait:

- *It will involve your single greatest strength.* Whatever your life work turns out to be, it will maximize your single greatest strength.

- *You will love it!* When you find your life work, you will do that work even if no one pays you for it. "I read a sign when I was twenty years old that said, 'An activity is only work when you would rather be doing something else.'"

- *You never tire of it!* You may get tired doing your life work, but you never tire of the result. I get tired and fatigued consulting, but I never tire of the beauty I see when people begin to have clarity instead of fogginess in their eyes.

- *Others affirm you in this niche.* Maybe many things done in the past just didn't seem to fit. Friends who are open and honest might say, "I don't think you will be doing this long. I don't think it's really you." However, when we find our life work, we will find our closest friends saying, "Aha! You have now found your true niche."

- *You earn an adequate income to make a living.* Many artists would like to have painting, acting, or singing be their life work, but if you asked them if they could make a living at it, they would say, "Oh, no, it's more like a hobby." In order to qualify as a life work, you must be able to make a living doing it (or be financially independent to do it without needing money).

- *It is a significant use of the rest of your life. Fulfillment,* or rather the lack of it, is probably the single greatest buzz-word for people who are trying to sort out their life work. The lack of fulfillment is the reason $500,000-per-year exec-utives resign from corporate America and teach college for $40,000.

As you look ahead to twenty or thirty years of active ser-vice, it's critical to be able to conclude that what you are doing is the best use of your life. You must conclude that this work would be a worthy use, a noble use, a "highest good" use of your life, or you will know your current career is not your life work.[10]

Let me make a couple of recommendations.

- If you are interested in finding out more about your strengths as a man and a father, then I would highly rec-ommend Bobb's booklet on Life Work (you can order it directly from Master Planning Associates by calling 800-443-1976).
- If you are interested in some tools that will give you a head start in understanding the strengths of each of your chil-dren, then get a copy of *Different Children, Different Needs: The Art of Adjustable Parenting,* by Charles F. Boyd. This biblically sound book is exactly the jump start you need to understand your children's strengths. It is the one indis-pensable tool that will enable you to do what we've been discussing this entire chapter.

BENT ON BENTS

And how long do you teach your kids? How long do you train a child? The whole time he is under your roof. The Hebrew word for "child" that is used in Proverbs 22:6 can mean an infant or it can mean a young boy who is beginning to sprout some whiskers. So you "train up a child in the way he should go" from the time he is a baby until he can look you in the eye. As long as he is in your home, it is the father's job to encourage his child in the direction of his strengths.

How do you discover what your child's strengths are? You obviously spend time with that child. You get to know that child. You get an advanced degree in that child. You know that child like you know the back of your hand. You *understand* that child. And you help that child to begin to understand himself. Once you get a read on his or her strengths, then encourage your child to work on those strengths.

For years and years the Chinese have been the best Ping-Pong players in the world. In 1984, they predictably won the gold medal at the Olympics. At the press conference, a reporter requested of the coach, "Please tell what you do to train your players."

The coach replied, "We practice eight hours a day perfecting our strengths."

The reporter asked if the coach could give him more specifics.

"Here is our philosophy: If you develop your strengths to the maximum, the strength becomes so great it overwhelms the weaknesses. Our winning player, you see, plays *only* his forehand. Even though he cannot play backhand and his competition knows he cannot play backhand, his forehand is so invincible that it cannot be beaten."[11]

If you teach your children how to recognize their bents and strengths, then the bottom line is that they will live lives of fulfillment and contentment. Why will they be fulfilled and so content? Because they will be functioning in the area of their strengths. But that's not all. Because you taught them how to recognize their strengths, they will probably teach their children how to recognize theirs. And they will live lives of fulfillment and contentment when they become adults because they, too, are functioning in the way that God intended.

So there it is again. Teach your children about their God-given bents and strengths and they will be productive citizens of the kingdom of God. And so will their children. Once again, you've provided them leadership that will last for a hundred years. And when you meet them in heaven, they will thank you for it.

—8—

BRAVEHEART

"Every man dies . . . but not every man lives."

—William Wallace

Where were you in 1970? It really wasn't that long ago . . . just twenty-eight years. It's hard to believe but back in 1970,

- there were no VCRs.
- there were no video camcorders.
- there were no pocket calculators.
- there were no Walkmen.
- there were no fax machines.
- there were no personal computers.
- there were no personal copiers.
- there were no compact discs.
- there were no cellular phones.

I'm writing these words on my Powerbook laptop computer at 32,000 feet as I'm headed from Dallas to Charlotte. Yet just twenty-eight years ago, none of these things existed. No laptops, no faxes, no cell phones.

If we stay on the track we are currently on, twenty-eight years from now there will be no fathers.

Don't misunderstand me. There will always be men around who will gladly impregnate a woman. In that sense, there will be biological fathers. But I'm talking about the kind of father who will not just conceive a child, but will raise that child. I'm talking about the kind of father who stays married to the mother of his children and provides, protects, and leads his family. Twenty-eight years from now, those kinds of fathers will be a distinct and rare minority.

Every once in a while I'll see some guy on the freeway driving a '57 Chevy or a '65 Mustang. Everybody on the freeway slows down just a little to take a closer look. You don't see many of those around anymore. Twenty-eight years from now, when people see a father living in the same house with his wife and children, they are going to slow down and take a long look. And someone will say, "Yeah, there sure aren't many of those around anymore."

I like the way Chuck Swindoll put it a while back:

> Remember when men were men?
>
> Remember when you could tell by looking?
>
> Remember when men knew who they were, liked how they were, and didn't want to be anything but what they were?
>
> Remember when it was the men who boxed and wrestled and bragged about how much they could bench press?
>
> Remember when it was the women who wore the makeup, the earrings, and the bikinis?
>
> Remember when it was the men who initiated the contact and took the lead in a relationship, made lifelong commitments, and modeled a masculinity grounded in security and stability?[1]

I recently came across a letter from a sixteen-year-old girl to her father. Just the week before, her father had come home and announced to his family that he was leaving them to move in with another woman. His wife and three children were in absolute shock. This guy was a churchgoing, solid citizen who had been happily married for nineteen years. And without warning, he walked in one night and destroyed everything that he and his wife had been carefully building for nearly two decades.

I would ask you to read this letter from his daughter slowly. She is a very articulate young lady. And she is a very intelligent young lady. She is also a grieving young lady. Listen to her reasoning as she tries to communicate with a father who is emotionally murdering his family. Listen as she attempts to find some common ground with her dad that will enable her to get into his mind and heart. I've been given permission to share her letter, but of course the names have been changed to protect the family's privacy:

Daddy,

I know that you were a really good football player. I can just picture the fans cheering for you. I would have been cheering, too, if I were there. What our family is going through now is kind of like a ball game.

This is the most important game. It is the championship game and everything rests on its outcome. You are the captain of our team and Tommy [her fourteen-year-old brother] is on the team. I am cheering for you on the sidelines. Mom and Ashley are the other cheerleaders. We are cheering for you, believing and trusting that you will do your best to not let us down. You have already done so much for us.

We have such a great team. We have tons of fans that love our team. They respect us and look up to us. They are always there for us, cheering us on.

Daddy, then something terrible happens in the game. When the play is run, there is a terrible collision of both teams on the sideline. We all got knocked down. It surprised us so badly. Many people were hurt. The players were slow getting up. The crowd was yelling. All of the cheerleaders were still down. Ashley has a broken leg. She was just lying there, still in shock. She didn't understand how this could happen to her wonderful team.

We had just been playing such a wonderful game. I was hit in the stomach and I can't catch my breath to call for help. I want to so badly though. Not being able to catch my breath makes my heart hurt. Pain is piercing all over my body. Mom is really hurt bad. She was crushed by one of the players. Several ribs were broken. One of them punctured her lungs and almost pierced her heart. I can barely tell if she's alive. She has taken the worst hit of all of us.

When the teams went back to the huddle, something very strange happened to you. It seems like you have hit your head really badly. I think you have a concussion. You are confused and can't see very well. You are walking around dazed. We were all watching you walk back to the huddle, but Daddy, you are going to the wrong huddle! You are walking to the wrong team! Tommy is yelling for you. He said, "Daddy, here we are over here!" All of your fans are screaming at you, saying, "Eric, come back to your team! You have to come back or we will lose the game." Ashley cries, "Daddy, can't you hear us?"

We need you on our team so badly. You must not hear us because you went to the other team. They start to do better for a while. Our team doesn't know what to do without you. Tommy is trying so hard, but he still needs you to coach him on the plays. Someone from our team says, "Where is your dad? Doesn't he know he is on the wrong team? We don't know what to do without him."

I am looking for help everywhere. I can't help Mom or Ashley on my own because I am hurt so badly myself. I see an ambulance, but I don't know who has the keys. We are still on the field, cold and lonely. Mama is hurt so bad. Why doesn't help come?

- We need help for you, because you are confused and you have gone to the other team.
- We need help for Tommy, who is lost without you there to know what calls he should make.

- We need help for Ashley, who can't understand what happened to her wonderful team.
- We need help for me, I am so sad. I don't have a reason to cheer without you.
- And we need help for Mom, who may die because *all* she has ever worked for in her life is this team. She has put everything into it, and now all of a sudden she is robbed of it. She has no reason to go on living.

That is why I pray for help. Where could the help be?

Daddy, you are the only one who can help. You have the keys to the ambulance. You are the only one who can pick us up off the field and nurse us back to health. Can't you realize that? We need you.

I know you are hurt, Daddy. We want to help you because we still love you so much. We want you back on our team, please, Daddy! I am begging you. We can all help each other. That is what a family is for.

It is halftime. You have to make your decision soon. You have to know you can't play for both teams. It just won't work. Which team are you going to be the captain of? The team you created that loves you more than anything or the team that confused you and made you think you were on the right team?

I wish I could do something to help you make the right decision. I would even *die* to save my daddy.

I am praying for you because I love you. Please do what it takes to come home and stay with us.

Your daughter,
Me.

This young girl is pleading with her father to have a brave heart.

But unfortunately for her and her family, her father has a faint heart.

I don't know the circumstances that prompted her father to abandon them. But I imagine somewhere in his thinking was the concept that he needed his "freedom."

That sixteen-year-old girl has a broken heart. Her mother has a broken heart. Her brother and sister have broken hearts.

And why does this family have broken hearts? It's very clear-cut. This family is full of broken hearts because the man of their family is lacking a brave heart.

The principle is simple yet profound: *Men who don't develop brave hearts break hearts.*

When the battery in my Powerbook ran out of juice at 32,000 feet, I picked up the *New York Times* that was in the empty seat next to me. I read a short article on a very successful American novelist. This woman is in her early forties. Her income last year from her numerous best-sellers was seventeen *million* dollars. But by her own admission, her life has been a mess. After her father abandoned her family when she was five, her mother placed the children in a foster home and checked herself into a mental hospital. As a teenager, she suffered from anorexia. In college, she became infatuated with a professor whom she married when she graduated. She has suffered severe mood swings most of her adult life, been hooked on alcohol for more years than not, and recently survived a car accident that occurred after she drank an entire pitcher of Bloody Marys. She was cut from the wreckage with the jaws of life. In addition to all of this, the husband of her new lesbian lover tried to murder his former wife when he learned of their affair.

As I mentioned earlier, her father abandoned her when she was five years old. He left home on Christmas Day to move in with his secretary, who was pregnant. Can you imagine how self-centered a guy has to be to abandon his family on *Christmas Day*? Christmas Day is the most important day of the year in the life of a five-year-old girl. Her father crushed her heart and killed her spirit on that particular day. But apparently, he was willing to sacrifice his daughter so that he, too, could find "freedom." Her own words tell the story:

> I was at that age when little girls worship their daddies. It killed me. It absolutely killed me. I remember him coming out into the hallway. I knew immediately what he was doing. He was never coming back. I ran over crying and screaming and wrapped around one of his legs like a little tree frog and I was screaming "Don't go! Don't go!" He kind of put me off. He didn't say anything. He just went out the door . . . I used to walk to the post office on holidays and my birthday, several times a day, hoping for mail, or gifts. But nothing ever came.[2]

Do you think that the fact that this woman has struggled with anorexia, alcohol, divorce, and homosexuality has anything to do with the fact that her father abandoned her on Christmas Day when she was five years old? I do.

May I suggest a root cause for this woman's lifelong troubles? Her father did not have a brave heart.

You see, like the sixteen-year-old girl, this forty-one-year-old woman has a broken heart. Her mother has a broken heart. Her brother, now a medical doctor, has a broken heart. And the reason that all of their hearts were broken was that the husband and father in their family did not have a brave heart. He thought he had to find his own personal "freedom."

If you saw the movie *Braveheart,* then you know the story of William Wallace. William Wallace is probably the greatest hero of Scotland. Until the movie *Braveheart,* most Americans had never heard of Wallace. But his life and legend have been strong in Scotland for nearly seven hundred years.

William Wallace was a committed Christian. The movie touched on his faith but diluted his Christianity by inserting immorality that historically has no basis. In actuality, Wallace was so serious about his faith that he had a personal chaplain, a man by the name of John Blair, who traveled with him at all times.[3] Blair was the man who wrote the original history of William Wallace. Blair's account of Wallace's life was eventually lost, but a blind man with a prolific memory had memorized the account and traveled around Scotland, reciting the story of William Wallace.

Wallace was born somewhere around 1267. The king of Scotland died without leaving a male heir to be crowned king. The king of England, Edward the Longshanks, stepped in while Scotland was without a leader and claimed Scotland for England. He paid off the Scottish nobles with huge grants of land and additional titles to get them to agree to his claim. William Wallace refused to go along with this arrangement. He wanted Scotland to be free. He was tired of English soldiers raping, murdering, and pillaging the common families of Scotland. They even killed Wallace's wife, Murron. So single-handedly, he rallied the common men of Scotland to fight against the armies of England.

For a time, Wallace was able to unite even the greedy nobles against England. But eventually their selfishness motivated them to betray William Wallace. Wallace, facing overwhelming opposition from the English, defeated them in several key battles. He then decided to do the impossible and invade England.

The king of England realized that William Wallace was a formidable and dangerous opponent. So the king offered Wallace money, land, and titles to gain his cooperation. Wallace refused. Unlike the nobles, he couldn't be bought. He had integrity. He believed in a higher principle than personal fulfillment. William Wallace wanted freedom for all of the people of Scotland. William Wallace had a brave heart.

If you saw the movie, then you remember the young noble, Robert the Bruce. He was the logical successor to become the next king of Scotland. His father, who was thought to be away fighting in France, was actually in the castle tower, where he was dying of leprosy. The old man was one of the treacherous nobles who was cooperating with the king of England.

Young Robert the Bruce was taken with the passion and courage of William Wallace. In a dialogue with Wallace, Robert argues that they must seek the cooperation of the nobles. Wallace replies, "What does it mean to be noble? Your title gives you the right to the throne of our country. But people don't follow titles. They follow courage."

Those words pierced Robert's heart like arrows. After meeting Wallace, he decided to join in alliance with him against the king of England. But shortly thereafter, his father convinced him otherwise. His father, realizing his admiration of Wallace, advises his son, "Admire this man, this William Wallace. Uncompromising men are easy to admire. He has courage, but so does a dog. *But it is exactly the ability of a man to compromise that makes him noble.*"

What a warped view of nobility. This guy would have been right at home with the majority of politicians. And he would have been right at home with a lot of guys who walk out on their families.

Thinking he has Robert's support, Wallace soon goes into battle against Longshanks and his army, convinced that Robert will join him at any minute. As Wallace gazes across the battlefield, what he doesn't know is that the masked knight, astride his horse next to the king of England, is Robert the Bruce. Robert had been convinced by his deceitful father to betray William Wallace.

During the battle, Robert, disguised as the masked knight, is dispatched to kill Wallace, who is madly dashing on his horse to kill Longshanks as he leaves the battlefield. He manages to knock Wallace off of his horse, and as Robert approaches the deathly still Wallace to turn his body over,

Wallace pulls him down, throws off his helmet, and puts a knife to his throat. It is at this moment that Wallace realizes it is Robert the Bruce. And that Robert has betrayed him. In shock from betrayal and from the loss of blood from an earlier wound, he is spirited away by one of his men to safety.

Robert the Bruce retches from his betrayal of William Wallace. He is physically ill from his deceit of such a decent man. He realizes that he is a Judas.

When he returns to his father, whose face is rotting because of leprosy, the father says: "I'm the one who's face is rotting, but your face looks graver than mine."

The young Robert replies in anguish, "I have nothing. Men fight for me, because if they do not, I throw them off my land and I starve their wives and children. Those men who bled the ground red at Falkirk, they fought for William Wallace, and he fights for something that I've never had. And I took it from him when I betrayed him and I saw it in his face on the battlefield, and it's tearing me apart."

His father then utters some remarkable words: "Well, all men betray. All lose heart."

And the son replies, "I don't want to lose heart. I want to believe as he does. I will never be on the wrong side again."

Not all men betray. And not all men lose heart. But never in the history of the world have so many fathers voluntarily betrayed their families. That's why it is no exaggeration to say that in twenty-eight years there may be no fathers.

There are not many bravehearts left. But there are many who are faint of heart. But that is nothing new. The bravehearts have always been in the minority. Today, we call that minority of bravehearts Christian fathers.

There will always be Christian fathers.

Christian fathers are different.

Christian fathers don't abandon their families.

Christian fathers don't leave when things get tough.

Christian fathers don't do impulsive, self-centered things that destroy their homes. Other fathers may do those things. But not Christian fathers.

Christian fathers are not faint of heart.

Christian fathers are brave-hearted.

Christian fathers protect their families.

Christian fathers take responsibility for their families.

Don't get me wrong. Christian fathers make their share of mistakes. They lose their tempers from time to time and they say things that they later regret. That's because they are not perfect. But when they do things that are wrong toward their wives or children they move quickly to repair the damage. They are swift to ask forgiveness and to do everything within their power to make things right.

Everywhere that you look in this nation, you will see fewer and fewer men with brave hearts. And you will see fewer churches with bravehearts in the pulpit. I was on the phone yesterday with the pastor of a very large and prominent church. I was calling him to turn down an invitation that had been extended to me to speak to the men of his congregation. The reason that I was turning down the invitation was that he had a well-known former pastor address his congregation the week before. The reason this very gifted man is a former pastor is that he decided to leave his wife and children and marry his secretary.

I was explaining to this pastor that it made no sense for me to come and talk to his men about being faithful husbands and fathers when he would put up before his men a man who had betrayed his wife and family and had not repented of what he had done. I told him that I would never speak in his church because I did not want to give the impression that I condoned this other man's actions.

This pastor had a hard time understanding my reasoning. Finally I said, "I understand you've been encouraging your men to go to Promise Keepers. What I don't understand is why you would invite a promise breaker to teach your men."

"But, Steve, the Bible was written by men who failed greatly. Men like David and Peter. I see no reason for us not to extend grace to this man."

"There's one big difference between David and Peter and this guy. David and Peter repented of their sin. When they sinned, they repented and they repented publicly. This guy hasn't repented. If he had repented, both of us would know about it. But he hasn't repented over his sin and apparently he hasn't wept over his sin. That's why it's a grave error to put him in front of your men. Before anyone can receive grace and mercy, they must first repent. That's the difference. When he repents, I'll be first in line to shake his hand and welcome him back."

Perhaps you are reading this and saying, "It is too late for me. I have already left my wife and children. I abandoned them in a moment of weakness. I betrayed my family as Robert the Bruce betrayed William Wallace." It isn't too late. Not if you will turn from your sin and run back to Christ.

I heard of a man just last week who had been suckered into an affair with another woman. He had left his family and moved in with this woman. He had betrayed his family. But a couple of his friends went and talked with him. And they started at the very beginning. They didn't ask him how he felt about his wife, they asked him about where he was with Jesus Christ. "Do you really know Christ as your Lord and Savior?" was the first question out of their mouths. And he said, "Believe it or not, I do. I know that I do." Then they said, "Then you can't do this. It doesn't fit and it doesn't make any sense. It is contrary to everything that you stand for as a Christian." By the end of the evening, he had packed up his things and gone back home.

These guys were smart. They began at the beginning. They asked him if he was sure that he was a Christian. And then he told them why he was sure that he was a Christian. And he gave them a biblical answer.

Not everyone who professes to be a Christian is a Christian.

Not every father who claims to be a Christian father is a Christian father.

John Piper recalls his conversation with a professing Christian husband and father who abandoned his family:

> I tried to understand his situation and I pled with him to return to his wife. Then I said, "You know, Jesus says if you don't fight this sin with the kind of seriousness that is willing to gouge out your own eye, you will go to hell and suffer there forever." As a professing Christian he looked at me in utter disbelief, as though he had never heard anything like this in his life, and said, "You mean you think a person can lose his salvation?"
>
> So I have learned again and again from firsthand experience that there are many professing Christians who have a view of salvation that disconnects it from real life, and that nullifies the threats of the Bible, and puts the sinning person who claims to be a Christian beyond the reach of biblical warnings. I believe this view of the Christian life is comforting thousands who are on the broad way that leads to destruction (Matthew 7:13). Jesus said, "If you don't fight lust, you won't go to heaven." Not that saints always succeed. The issue is that we resolve to fight, not that we succeed flawlessly.[4]

So what's the difference between a father who is a Christian and a father who claims to be a Christian? The difference is that the genuine Christian father will fight against lust and wrong thoughts. He is not always successful, but on the other hand, he doesn't invite wrong thoughts into his life either. The professing Christian doesn't want to fight. He enjoys the sin too much. But the man who is a genuine Christian can't enjoy the sin. Oh, he might get a kick or two out of it for a few minutes. But then the enjoyment is crowded out by a tremendous sense of conviction. And why is he convicted about his sin? Because the Holy Spirit lives in the heart of every man who genuinely knows Christ.

Maybe, like Robert the Bruce, you've been on the wrong side. Perhaps you haven't left your family, but you have secretly been hitting on pornographic web sites on the Internet when your wife and children are asleep. In a couple of minutes, you can visit pornographic sites that are absolutely beyond belief in their evilness and wickedness. And a man can do it all in the privacy of his own home. And he's all by himself. Or at least he thinks he is.

Or perhaps it's not the Internet. Maybe it's phone sex. American men spent close to $1 billion last year on sex over the phone. Or maybe you've visited a "gentlemen's club" when you were away from home on business. This stuff is everywhere. And it's available in ways that most of us would never think possible. It's easier than ever before to have private sexual sin. But private sexual sin is betrayal. And it is robbing you of a brave heart for your family.

> **I will lead a life of integrity in my own home. I will refuse to look at anything vile and vulgar. I hate all crooked dealings; I will have nothing to do with them. I will reject perverse ideas and stay away from every evil.** (Ps. 101:2–4 NLT)

You wouldn't be reading this book if you didn't want to be a godly father. That's exactly what you want! Secret sin gives the enemy a foothold in your life. Secret sin lets him control you and intimidate you. Secret sin lets him deal the cards.

Do you know what the enemy is doing when he lures you into this secret sin, this private sin? Let me tell you what he is up to. Private sin eventually leads to public sin.

I referred earlier in this chapter to two men who had abandoned their families. I guarantee you there was unchecked private sin in both of their lives before they made the public break from their families. That's how it always happens. And that's where Satan wants to eventually take you . . . from the private sin to the public sin.

The Scriptures tell us that we can be sure that our sin will find us out. The sin we commit in private will some day come out. It will be made public. That will dishonor you, your family, and your Lord. So why not deal with it now? If you are in secret sin, in private sin, then you are feeling trapped.

How does a man who has become secretly trapped get out of the trap? That's the big-time question.

James, the half brother of Jesus, laid out a prescription: "Confess your trespasses to one another, and pray for one another, that you may be healed. The effective, fervent prayer of a righteous man avails much" (James 5:16 NKJV).

When a Christian man gets into private sexual sin, the enemy wants you to think that he has all the exits covered. But that's not true. There is a way of escape.

The first thing that you must do is to confess your sin. The moment you confess a secret sin it is no longer a secret. As soon as you confess your sin, you immediately outflank the enemy. You outflank him because you are through covering up. You are done with living a lie. When you confess sin, you are admitting to sin. And some of you have done that many times. You have admitted your sin to the Lord, but before you know it, you are back into it. The reason we get back into secret sexual sin is that we normally forget a critical step in James's prescription.

James doesn't just say confess your sin . . . he says confess your sins to one another. Now I know what you're thinking. You're thinking that you couldn't ever do that. You are so embarrassed by your sin and you are so ashamed of your sin, that you could never tell someone else about it. It's one thing to admit it to God. It's another to admit it to a trusted friend. And this is where many of us get conned by the enemy. He convinces us that if we ever did admit our private sin to a close and trusted friend, then that friend would have nothing to do with us. Of course you don't want someone else to know, if he is going to reject you. But the fact of the matter is, a mature Christian friend won't reject you, he will embrace you. Satan is lying to you about what will happen if you confess your sin to a brother. And when we believe the lie, then we cut ourselves off from the exit that Christ has provided.

But you say, "Steve, I don't think I can do that. I'm just too ashamed. You don't know what I've done, you wouldn't believe what I've done." Yes, I would believe it. Anyone who's been in ministry for over twenty-five years isn't going to be shocked. Believe me, he has heard everything. And I mean everything.

Listen to me. I know that it's hard. But it must be done. Hey, if you found out tomorrow that you had a cancerous tumor, you would be in surgery to remove that tumor the next morning. Would that be hard? Of course it would. But you would do it because the only alternative is to let the tumor grow and take over the rest of your body. That's the way it is with secret sin. It's not going to shrink, it's going to grow. That tumor of secret sin isn't going to get better. It's going to get worse. Much worse. So you must find a godly, mature Christian man with whom you can come clean. James says that there is no other way.

You cannot coddle your sin.

You cannot pamper your sin.

You must get ruthless with your sin.

The first step to becoming a braveheart is to get brave about dealing with your sin. Believe me. There is no shortcut.

Here's the good news. You don't have to be enslaved to that secret sin any longer. And you don't have to serve sin any longer. Sin is not your master. Christ is your Master.

It is not too late for you. Not if you have a truly repentant heart. Not if with every fiber of your being you regret what you have done and confess that to the ultimate Braveheart, Jesus Christ. If that is your condition, then you can still become a braveheart. Just as Robert the Bruce did.

William Wallace was finally captured. He was on his way to a secret meeting with the repentant Robert the Bruce when the other nobles betrayed him into the hands of Longshanks.

At his trial, William Wallace was given the option of confessing his allegiance to the king and gaining a swift death, or refusing to submit and undergoing a cruel and slow death. He chose the latter.

In a gripping scene, alone in prison and preparing to face the torture of being racked and disemboweled, Wallace prayed to his Lord: "I am so afraid. Give me the strength to die well."

And he did.

Even when his body was stretched out of joint, he did not cry out. Even when he was tied down to a wooden cross and disemboweled, he did not cry out. But with his last dying breath, before he was beheaded, he finally cried out. Mustering every resource that was left in his broken and mutilated body, he cried out, "Freeeeeeeedom!"

Freedom. There's that word again. William Wallace had a passion for freedom. But Wallace's passion was for a different kind of freedom from that of the men who abandon their families.

Donald Wildmon describes it well:

> What is freedom? Well, never make the mistake of thinking that freedom is a matter of rights. It isn't. It is a matter of right. And no man can become free until he has become a slave to something higher and greater than himself.[5]

In the final scene of *Braveheart,* Robert the Bruce is once again lined up with his men on one side of a large open tract of land facing the army of England. William Wallace has died after refusing to bow allegiance to the king of England, and being racked and disemboweled. Only this time, they are not there for battle. They are there for peace. They have all gathered to witness Robert the Bruce signing the agreement that promises his continued cooperation and submission to the king of England. Many of the men who fought with William Wallace are gathered behind Robert the Bruce. They have lost their leader and their new leader is getting ready to go to the wrong huddle. But something happens.

As Robert nudges his horse to cross the field and sign the agreement that will secure what is best for him and subjugate the people of Scotland for another generation, he suddenly stops. He then turns to the men of Scotland, looks them over from head to toe, and says, "You bled for Wallace. Now bleed for me."

And with that he draws his sword and leads his men in attacking the army of England. And under Robert the Bruce, the former betrayer, Scotland gained its freedom.

Robert the Bruce kept the promise that he uttered to his father: "I don't want to lose heart. I want to believe as he does. I will never be on the wrong side again."

With his words and his actions, Robert the Bruce changed. He once was a betrayer, a cowardheart. He became a braveheart. So can you.

It was said of David that he shepherded Israel according to the integrity of his heart. It should be said of Christian fathers that they shepherded their families according to the integrity of their hearts. David was not a man without flaws. He betrayed his God with his sexual sin with Bathsheba. But David was a braveheart. He was a man after God's own heart.

There is only one thing that will stop the erosion of fathering in America. It is a change of heart. A heart that changes from being self-serving to becoming Christ-serving. That's what will make the difference.

You can have a new Master. A Master who is kind, forgiving, and loving. A Master who can make you into the kind of man and father you really want to be. You don't have to serve that old, decrepit master of sin anymore. No matter what you have done, you can join the millions of other men who have found true freedom, not by claiming your rights, but by doing what is right. And the right thing to do is to give your life entirely to Christ. Throw yourself on His mercy, ask His forgiveness, and ask Him to create in you a new heart.

A clean heart; a forgiven heart.

Then you, too, will be a braveheart.

—9—

MEMORIAL STONES

"The great doers of history have always been men of faith."

—Edwin Hubbel Chapin

It was just a pile of stones. But it was there because God ordered it. Just twelve stones piled up one on top of the other. But never have twelve stones been more important. A group of fathers had carefully placed the stones by the river. Were the stones to be used to build a wall? Were the stones to be used to build a house? The answer to both questions is no. The stones were to be used to build a new civilization. A civilization of faith in the mighty God of Israel.

When the fathers of Israel, along with their families, finally crossed over into the promised land, they crossed on dry land. What's the big deal about that? Of course they would walk on dry land to get to their new home. The big deal is this. They walked on dry land where just seconds before there had been a raging, roaring river that had crested above flood stage. This river was a mile wide, it was 150 feet deep. And in an instant, as soon as the priest's foot touched the water, this river obeyed its Creator and rolled itself back to a divinely mandated boundary.

Where treacherous water had been flowing just seconds before, there now was no water. And not only was there no water, there was no evidence that water had *ever* been there. There was no dampness. Absolutely none. And there was no mud. The land beneath the river was made instantaneously as dry as an abandoned acre in the middle of Death Valley.

As the Jordan River submitted to the command of its Master, the men of Israel crossed over this now dry riverbed with their families. The priests, who were carrying the ark of the covenant on their shoulders, led everyone into the water. When they got halfway across the path the loyal river had just vacated, they stopped, while the two million people of Israel crossed to the other side.

God told Joshua in advance that He was going to do this. Forty years before He had also rolled back the Red Sea for Moses; now He was going to do it for Joshua to validate his leadership as Moses' successor:

> **Behold, the ark of the covenant of the Lord of all the earth is crossing over ahead of you into the Jordan. Now then, take for yourselves twelve men from the tribes of Israel, one man for each tribe. And it shall come about when the soles of the feet of the priests who carry the ark of the LORD, the Lord of all the earth, shall rest in the waters of the Jordan, the waters of the Jordan shall be cut off, and the waters which are flowing down from above shall stand in one heap. . . . And the priests who carried the ark of the covenant of the LORD stood firm on dry ground in the middle of the Jordan while all Israel crossed on dry ground, until all the nation had finished crossing the Jordan.**

(Josh. 3:11–13, 17)

This is where the twelve men that Joshua chose from each tribe were put to work:

> **Now it came about when all the nation had finished crossing the Jordan, that the LORD spoke to Joshua, saying, "Take for yourselves twelve men from the people, one man from each tribe, and command them, saying, 'Take up for yourselves twelve stones from here out of the middle of the Jordan, from the place where the priests' feet are standing firm, and carry them over with you, and lay them down in the lodging place where you will lodge tonight.'" So Joshua called the twelve men whom he had appointed from the sons of Israel, one man from each tribe; and Joshua said to them, "Cross again to the ark of the LORD your God into the middle of the Jordan, and each of you take up a stone on his shoulder, according to the number of the tribes of the sons of Israel.**
> **"Let this be a sign among you, so that when your children ask later, saying, 'What do these stones mean to you?' then you shall say to them, 'Because the waters of the Jordan were cut off before the ark of the covenant of the LORD; when it crossed the Jordan, the waters of the Jordan were cut off.' So these stones shall become a memorial to the sons of Israel forever."** (Josh. 4:1–7)

There were actually two piles of stones. Twelve stones were placed in the middle of the Jordan River. When the river was low, the pile of twelve stones could be clearly seen from the bank. It has been pointed out that for the river to be this low, the nation definitely was in need of rainfall. But the stones in the middle of a low river were a reminder that God had been faithful in the past and that He would again be faithful in the future.

The second pile of stones we have already been introduced to. Twelve men of Israel, undoubtedly twelve fathers of Israel, walked out to the middle of the dry Jordan and each of them hoisted a good-size rock on his shoulder and brought it over to where they would camp. That area was known as Gilgal. They stacked the twelve stones on top of one another at Gilgal. The entire purpose of these memorial stones was to instruct the children of each future generation of the faithfulness of God. Francis Schaeffer described the scenario well:

> We can imagine a godly Jew in years to come taking his children to the twelve stones in Gilgal and saying, "Look! These stones were taken up out of the Jordan. I was there. I saw it happen." Then the grandfather would tell the grandchild, and, though the people died off, the story would go on.[1]

The text states that God commanded these fathers to construct this pile of stones as "a sign among you, so that when your children ask later, saying, 'What do these stones mean to you?' . . ." God wanted those memorial stones set up so that the kids of Israel would ask their dads about them. Here's the purpose of memorial stones: *They are reminders of the greatness and goodness of God to those who choose to follow Him with their whole hearts.*

When the men of Israel were to cross into the promised land, a swift and swollen river was blocking their path. But the God who controls all things, including His rivers, provided for the future of those men and their families by pushing back the river and drying the ground.

Memorial stones are signs of God's providence in our lives. When we run into difficulties and hardships, we count on God's providence to take care of us in the same way that He took care of His people as they faced the Jordan River. Generally speaking, when we speak of God's providence we are referring to the fact that God controls all things in His creation and He is the One who provides for our future.

Have you ever been to Providence, Rhode Island? Believe it or not, that city is a memorial stone to the goodness and grace of God. The founder of that city was Roger Williams. If you remember your early American history, you remember that Roger Williams was thrown out of Massachusetts because his teachings were not popular. In 1636, he settled on some land that the Indians gave to him. He named the new settlement Providence, because he believed that God had led him there to provide for his future.

PERSONAL MEMORIAL STONES

Over the years, Mary and I have pulled out various memorial stones and shown them to our children. We want them to know about how God's providence and goodness have worked in our lives.

- We have told them about God's providence in bringing us together in marriage. Do you have an album of wedding pictures? That's a memorial stone that you can pull out and show to your children.
- We have told them about God's providence in using times of hardship and disappointment to lead us in a new direction (more about that later).
- We have told them about God's providence in times of crisis.

Less than a mile from our home, there is another house that is a memorial stone for our family. My brother, Mike, and his family used to live in that house. We had spent nearly an entire summer afternoon in Mike's pool. We were going to have a quick dinner and then the four of us were going out to see a movie. I had just finished changing Josh's diaper and I walked back into the bedroom to see why the other kids were making so much noise. I spent about two minutes calming them down and then I went down the hallway to get my car keys. Suddenly, I stopped dead in my tracks: *Where is Josh?* That question hit me like a ton of bricks. I abruptly and unexpectedly had a tremendous sense of urgency. I took a few more steps down the hallway to see if Josh was in the family room. That's when I saw that the back door that led out to the pool was slightly ajar. And it was at that moment that I saw Josh at the bottom of the pool.

I yelled, "Mike!" and I went through that back door at about 60 miles an hour. I took two giant leaps and was in that pool faster than you would have believed. In one swoop, I reached down, grabbed Josh, and brought him straight up out of the water. He immediately spit water and started crying. And then I spit water and started crying. There I was, fully clothed, holding my little two-year-old boy in the pool. I thought I had lost him. But I hadn't.

Josh is now thirteen. And for as long as he can remember, he has known that story. Was it just coincidence that I suddenly became aware that I didn't know where Josh was? Was it coincidence that I became aware then and not five minutes later? It wasn't coincidence. It was the Holy Spirit who stopped me in my tracks. Why? Because He has a providential plan that He is going to accomplish in Josh's life. And every time we drive by that house, Josh sees a four-bedroom memorial stone to the goodness of God in his life.

If you are a man who loves Christ, there are memorial stones in your life as well. In days gone by, God has done some remarkable things for you. In fact, He has done some absolutely astonishing things for you. Those acts of God are your memorial stones. And your children need to know about them.

Several years ago, I was driving my family through the neighborhood in Bakersfield, California, that I grew up in as a young boy. I showed them all of the houses that I lived in as a boy, and I lived in quite a few. My dad built homes, and oftentimes we would live in a house for a year and then sell it and move just down the street into a brand-new home that my dad had just finished. I never changed schools but it was not uncommon for us to move every year or so.

I was showing them one of my favorite houses, the one on Kingston Drive. We used to go racing down that sloped street at speeds that seemed over a hundred miles an hour in the wooden coaster my dad built for us. As we slowed down in front of that house, I pointed out the corner window. That was my bedroom, and it was in that bedroom one night when I was seven that I asked Christ to come into my life.

My cousins had been over that day for a barbecue. And that night after dinner, when all of the kids had been put to bed, my mom and dad, along with my aunt and uncle, gathered around the piano in the living room. Years before they had been a traveling singing group and they were singing some of the old hymns of the church that they used to do together. All of the other kids were asleep, but I was still awake. And as I lay there in that bed, listening to the music, I started to listen to the words of the hymns. I began to realize as I listened to each verse that I was a sinner. I knew that I had sin in my heart and as each song was sung there was a growing sense of conviction in my heart. My sin had separated me from God. I was only seven years old, but my need of Christ was as real to me that night as it would ever be.

With tears running down my cheeks, I got up and opened the door and called for my dad. He was used to me getting up for unnecessary reasons, so he simply said, "Go back to bed." But then he and Mom saw that I had been crying. They asked me what was wrong and I said that I had been listening to the words of the songs and I needed to become a Christian. My mom and dad came into my room and we knelt by the bed. Dad told me about how Jesus had died on the cross to pay for my sin. He spent several minutes explaining to me how I could know Christ personally and have my sins forgiven. Together we prayed and then I prayed and asked Jesus to forgive me and to come into my life. That night changed my life forever. And as we were parked in front of that house, I told my kids that story. I was able to show them a memorial stone and tell them what God had done for me in that house many years ago.

You've got memorial stones in your life. It's important that, at the right time, you pull out those memorial stones and show them to your kids. According to Deuteronomy 6, fathers are to diligently teach their children the truth about God. And there is no better way to do that than by showing your kids a memorial stone. Your kids will remember the story of that memorial stone forever.

I recently read the following account of a man whose father was a traveling evangelist. He was recounting a memorial stone experience that happened over forty years ago. Back when this boy was growing up, his parents didn't have a year-round salary. They were dependent on the love offering that the church would give his father for holding a one- or two-week revival. I'll let him tell the story:

> I remember Dad going off to speak in a tiny church and coming home ten days later. My mother greeted him warmly and asked how the revival had gone. He was always excited about that subject. Eventually, in moments like this she would get around to asking him about the offering. Women have a way of worrying about things like that.
>
> "How much did they pay you?" she asked.
>
> I can still see my father's face as he smiled and looked at the floor. "Aw . . ." he stammered. My mother stepped back and looked into his eyes.
>
> "Oh, I get it," she said. "You gave the money away again, didn't you?"

"Myrt," he said. "The pastor there is going through a hard time. His kids are so needy. It just broke my heart. They have holes in their shoes and one of them is going to school without a coat. I felt I should give the entire fifty dollars to them."

My good mother looked intently at him for a moment and then she smiled. "You know, if God told you to do it, it's okay with me."

Then a few days later the inevitable happened. We ran completely out of money. There was no reserve to tide us over. That's when my father gathered us in the bedroom for a time of prayer. I remember that day as though it were yesterday. He prayed first.

"Oh, Lord, you promised that if we would be faithful with you and your people in our good times, then you would not forget us in our time of need. We have tried to be generous with what you have given us, and now we are calling on you for help."

A very impressionable ten-year-old boy named Jimmy was watching and listening very carefully that day. *What will happen?* he wondered. *Did God hear Dad's prayer?*

The next day an unexpected check for $1,200 came for us in the mail. Honestly! That's the way it happened, not just this once but many times. I saw the Lord match my dad's giving stride for stride. No, God never made us wealthy, but my young faith grew by leaps and bounds. I learned that you cannot outgive God.[2]

The man who told that story is the president of one of the largest ministries in the world. In order to do the work that God has called him to do in America and around the world, he and his staff must trust God to bring in millions of dollars each year. That takes a fair amount of faith! But as he saw his father trust God, James Dobson's faith grew and grew. That prayer of need from his father and God's answer of $1,200 was a memorial stone in the life of James Dobson.

And I'm sure that story thrilled his children when he passed it on to them.

A young college student knew the truth about Christ, but was really not interested in following Christ. He was enrolled in a Christian college but not making a lot of headway spiritually. He was calling his own shots instead of following Christ. He had the opportunity one summer to help build a new building for a small Christian medical clinic in the Middle East. Two Christian ladies had established this clinic literally on a prayer.

As this rebellious young man worked on the building with a friend, from time to time he would take a walk to have a smoke. And whenever he had an opportunity in the evening, he would take a shot of Jack Daniels. At this point in his life, he was not real interested in walking the straight and narrow. As far as he was from the Lord, he was quite impressed by these two ladies. He couldn't believe how they could run that clinic with no visible means of support. On numerous occasions that summer, they would pray before the evening meal that God would supply a certain need. These ladies did not send out a newsletter, and they did not make appeals. They simply trusted God. And it blew this college kid away. He tells the story of one prayer that became a memorial stone in his life:

> One Friday, Eleanor asked that we pray for the Lord to provide funds to pay a medicine bill from a Swedish company. I recall the gist of her plea:
>
>> Lord, You know that we don't have $1355, but this is Your hospital. Your name is on the line, not ours. If this bill doesn't get paid, it's Your name that gets discredited. If it pleases You, Lord, and if it be Your will, provide for this need. Amen.

I tried hard not to be cynical, but I couldn't believe that the money could come in if no one on the "outside" knew about the need. If they would just let their needs be known, maybe someone would care enough to help. I had grown to love these women, and I didn't want to see them hurt. But I had completely missed the point; they had already told Someone.

The next Monday an envelope arrived containing a hand-written note, which read: "I have heard about the wonderful work you are doing there, and you have been in my thoughts. I had some extra money and wanted to send it to you. Enclosed is a check. Use it any way you see fit."

The check was for $1,355.[3]

This young man had heard the gospel all of his life. He had heard his father, Billy Graham, preach the gospel many times. But the arrival of this check became a significant memorial stone in his young, rebellious heart. And it wasn't too long after he witnessed this remarkable answer to prayer, that he yielded his life to Christ. And that rebellious son, Franklin Graham, now preaches all over the world with his father. It all began with a $1,355 memorial stone. I'm sure that Franklin's children were thrilled when he passed that story on to them.

LATE ONE FRIDAY NIGHT

Several months ago, my daughter, Rachel, who is a senior in high school, came home after a football game. It was an away game and the bus that the cheerleading squad was coming home on had some trouble. She got in around midnight. Everyone else was in bed, but I had been waiting up for her. We were both pretty tired and ready to go to bed.

Rachel had missed dinner so she fixed a quick snack as I was scanning the sports page of the paper. As Rachel was eating, out of the blue, she asked, "Dad, how did you get into ministering to men?"

"Well, Rachel, that's sort of a long story."

"What I mean is, Dad, how did you actually go from pastoring a church for fifteen years to starting a ministry where you hold conferences for men? And when we moved to Dallas, how did we live? When you were at the church, the church paid you every month. But how did you get paid when you started this ministry?"

"Well, Rachel, Mom and I had to make a decision. When I wrote *Point Man,* there weren't too many books written for Christian men. And I was starting to get a lot of requests to speak to men in churches all over the country. But I had to turn most of the requests down because I was pastoring the church and couldn't be away. Several men that I had known for quite a while encouraged me to start a ministry that would focus on issues relating to men. This was back even before Promise Keepers got started, and hardly anyone was focusing on equipping men. But I wasn't sure I could launch a ministry to men and support our family. And I wasn't sure that God was really leading me to do this."

"So what made you finally decide to do it?" she asked.

"One morning, Mom and I were praying about this and I said to her, 'Mary, I'm not sure how we could get this off the ground financially. I have turned down all kinds of requests for the next six months and I've got nothing lined up. Quite frankly, I don't see how I could support a family for the next six months if we left the church. And it's my responsibility to make sure that we can make it. I know God doesn't want me doing something stupid. I don't want to do something that's going to put us in a big financial bind.'

"Mary said, 'Steve, if God is calling us to this new ministry, then He will provide the funds. What we must decide is if He is calling us to make this change, and if He is calling us, then He will provide a way to fund it. And I think He is calling us.'

"'I do, too, Mary. If you're willing to trust God with me, then let's go for it.'

"Rachel, that was the gist of our conversation that morning. We decided to go for it. But I have to confess that all morning I was wondering how this would work out. And then, a couple of hours later the phone rang. Do you remember when Mom was in that car accident at the shopping center? The guy who hit her was at fault. Mom hurt her neck and had about $5,000 in medical bills. The man's insurance company wanted me to sign a release form before they would pay the bills and, of course, I wouldn't do that. This went on for months and months and they wouldn't pay the doctors' bills. Finally, I asked a Christian attorney if he could help me get the $5,000 to pay the medical bills. I was wondering how we were going to make it for the next six months without any foreseeable income, when the attorney called. Now the accident had happened two and a half years before. But he called on that morning and asked me if I would settle for $24,000. I had never had $24,000 in my life. But by noon the next day, I deposited that check into our account."

Rachel said, "Dad, that's unbelievable."

I agreed. "You bet it is, Rachel. God was just letting us know that He knew our needs and that He was indeed calling us to this ministry."

"Rachel, do you remember when we first moved to Dallas, and the ministry 'headquarters' was upstairs in my study?"

"Sure I do, Dad. How long before you had an office and a secretary?"

"It was about a year. I just couldn't afford to hire a secretary. Our first year in Dallas was really interesting. Several individuals had heard about our new ministry and indicated that they would like to help get it off the ground financially.

I was doing speaking around the country but it wasn't usual for me to get a salary every month from the ministry. I never knew when someone was going to send a contribution to the ministry. I remember one month we needed $1,500 to come in so we could pay the bills at the first of the month. To tell you the truth, I was starting to wonder if God had really called me to start this new ministry.

"That morning I went out to the mailbox and there were two envelopes. In one was a check from some people who had heard what I was doing. They were writing to tell me that they were praying for me. Enclosed was a check to the ministry for $1,000. There was a note in the other envelope from some friends who also wanted to encourage us. They enclosed a check to the ministry too. How much was that check for, Rachel?"

"Five hundred?"

"Five hundred on the nose! God was letting me know again that He was with me."

At this point neither Rachel nor I was tired. We were both pumped.

"Do you remember when we set up that office and I hired Deedee? Well, just several months later, I was going out of town to speak. And I was really feeling a lot of pressure because on Monday, I had about $10,000 in bills that were due. We had a big printing bill for our brochures and manuals that was due, as well as office rent, and I needed to pay Deedee. And I was hoping that I could get paid too. As I left on Friday afternoon, we had $219 in the ministry checking account. I had no idea in the world how I was going to cover that $10,000.

"The next day, as I was getting ready to do my final session for the weekend, a man came up to me and put something in my pocket.

"'Steve, I'd like to make a small donation to your ministry. I wish I could do more. Thanks for what you are doing. Keep up the good work.'

"I mumbled a quick thank-you and quickly made my way to the platform to speak. Later as I was on my way to the airport, I remembered the check and thought that I better put it in my wallet so I wouldn't lose it. That's when I looked at it for the first time. How much was that check for, Rachel?"

"Ten thousand dollars?"

"That's exactly how much it was for."

Rachel said, "Dad, that's amazing!"

"Well, let me tell you another one. About a year later, I was doing a conference on the East Coast. It was our first conference of the winter. Rachel, this time the ministry had about $25,000 in bills. Here it was late January and we hadn't done a conference since Thanksgiving. With all of the activities between Thanksgiving and Christmas, and really for several weeks after January, it's not a good time to do conferences. Once again, I had another big printing bill. I was feeling the pressure and asking the Lord to bring in $25,000 so we wouldn't fall behind in our bills.

"After the conference, a couple invited me to dinner. As we were eating, the husband indicated how much the conference had meant to him personally. It covered some areas of conflict that he was wrestling with in his relationship with his own father. And out of the blue, he said that he and his wife had talked that afternoon about getting behind our ministry financially so that we could reach even more men. That's when he handed me a check and said, 'God has been very, very good to us. We'd like to pass His kindness on to your ministry, Steve.'

"When I got to my room, I opened the check. It was for $10,000. And I thought to myself, *Something's wrong.* Now don't misunderstand me. I was extremely grateful for the $10,000 but we needed to have $15,000 more. And then I thought to myself that if God could provide $10,000 out of the blue like that from a couple I had just met, then He could certainly provide the rest of the money in some other creative way.

"The next morning, this same couple were driving me to the airport. As we pulled up to the terminal, the husband said, 'You know, Steve, when we got home last night, neither one of us could sleep. Finally, I turned to my wife and said, "I'm not sure that we did everything that God wanted us to do." And she agreed.' And as I was getting out of the car to catch my flight, they handed me another check made out to the ministry.

"Rachel, how much was that check for?"

"It was for $15,000!"

"That's exactly right, Rachel. You're starting to catch on to this, aren't you?"

Rachel was excited to hear more and we stayed up for close to two hours. There were many other stories I told her that night of how God got our ministry off the ground. We experienced many times where, unless He came through, we were finished. But He always came through. Every single time.

DOWNSIZED FATHERS

Let me tell you the point of all of this. Over the last several years, as I have traveled around the country, I have met scores of Christian fathers who have lost their jobs. Corporations all over America are cutting back and downsizing. Highly capable and experienced men, who have been making good money and been with a company for ten, fifteen, or even twenty years, suddenly find themselves without a job. And it's difficult to get another job because most of the other companies are downsizing too. Just last week, I met three men, all very successful, who were the victims of downsizing.

It's tough to suddenly find yourself let go from a "secure" position. Especially when you've got three kids to take care of and one of them is in college, and two more are waiting to go to college. When a father finds out that his company is cutting back, and that he is part of the cut, that is an extremely traumatic experience. The tendency is to panic. What are we going to do? How will I provide for my family?

I have written this chapter for fathers who find themselves in that position. I have told you these stories for a reason. And the reason I have taken you through some of my experiences is that I want you to know that I have learned first-hand about the faithfulness of God.

Let me tell you something else. He knows your need. This downsizing you've experienced is not a surprise to Him. He knew it was coming before you were ever born. God is not shocked by it and He is not worried about it. As a matter of fact, He has ordained it and allowed it. He has not forgotten you, my friend. He knows exactly where you are and what you are going through. And He is getting ready to show you His greatness.

If you're like me, you love to hear stories of God's faithfulness. You love to hear how God has stepped in and met a need . . . in the life of someone else. We all like security. We like to know that check is going to be there every month. And quite frankly, that check becomes our security.

When a man is laid off, when a father gets downsized, it is a traumatic time. But may I give you a word of encouragement? You could be walking into one of the greatest experiences of your life. Listen, my friend, if you never have a need, then you never get to see the Lord do something great. We love to hear those great stories, but those great stories don't happen unless someone has a need! And you've got a need. So strap on your seat belt. You are in for the ride of your life.

And let me tell you something else. You are going to see the goodness of God. David said in Psalm 27:13, "I would have despaired, unless I had believed that I would see the goodness of the LORD." If God isn't there, then you are right to despair. But He is there! And He hasn't forgotten you or your family.

Some of you are going through the most difficult time of your lives financially. Let me offer you a bigger perspective than just paying your bills this month or next month. May I suggest to you that God is getting ready to give you some memorial stones? May I suggest to you that God is getting ready to take care of you in the same way He took care of Joshua and the people of Israel? God took care of a raging, rushing river. He loved those people so much that He took some extraordinary steps to tame that river so they could get across. What raging river are you facing today? Is that river at flood stage? Is it ten feet over flood stage?

You have the same God that Joshua had. You have the same God that Jim Dobson's father had. You have the same God that those two ladies who ran the medical clinic in the Middle East had, and you have the same God that I have.

Gentlemen, if we are always secure financially, if we always have money in the bank, if we always have everything we need, then, quite frankly, we miss out on some great blessings. Don't lose heart. God will give you what you need. And let me mention something else. God is big into "just-in-time" inventory.

In recent years, a number of corporations have gone to this "just-in-time" inventory concept. Instead of keeping big inventories in their warehouses, the shipments from their suppliers show up just a day or so before they actually need them.

Most businessmen don't know it, but God is the originator of "just-in-time" inventory. He has been doing it for thousands of years. He did it for Moses, He did it for Joseph, He did it for Elijah, and He's getting ready to do it for you. Do you have a need? Then God will meet your need. But He won't meet it until exactly the right time. You can count on it. It will be there just in time. Not before. Not after. Just in time.

And then, down the road, when you tell your kids the stories of God's faithfulness, they will say, "Dad, that's unbelievable!" And that memorial stone will be in your family chain for generations.

DRY COPIES

"It is not well for a man to pray cream and live skim milk."

—Henry Ward Beecher

Chester Carlson officially invented the photocopier on October 22, 1938. He had worked night and day for three years in a little rented room over a street-corner bar before he perfected his invention. And then the revolution began, right? Not quite. For years, Carlson tried to sell his invention. But nobody, and I mean nobody, was interested. He took it to IBM, Kodak, and RCA, and they all looked at him as if he were nuts. This was 1938, not 1998. One company president said, "Why would anybody want a copier? We already have carbon paper."

No one could see the need for a copier. For six solid years, Carlson pounded the pavement, trying to find a company that would invest in his invention. Finally, a small, research-oriented nonprofit institute bought a 60 percent interest in Carlson's invention. One of the researchers, who had studied Greek in college, coined a new word when he saw Carlson's copier. He came up with the word *xerography,* which roughly translated is "dry writing." Before long, another company came along and bought Carlson's technology. And eventually this company, the Haloid Corporation, changed its name to Xerox. And that's when the revolution began.

Today we can't imagine life without this "dry-writing" machine that produces "dry copies." We simply walk to our machine, put down an original, hit a button, grab the dry copy, and race on to our next task. In fact, I find myself getting a little irritated just waiting those interminable seconds it takes for the copy to emerge. But I wouldn't want to do without it.

Carlson was a creative genius. But his invention pales in light of the creative genius of God, for God created the technology for dry-copying people. How is it done? It is done through fathering. Like it or not, the old saying is true. Like father, like son.

My buddy Brent Lamb captured this so well in his song "Monkey See, Monkey Do":

Daddy's on the porch with an ice cold beer.
It sure gets hot this time of year.
Junior wants a drink 'cause he's thirsty, too.
Daddy, be careful . . . monkey see, monkey do.
Momma's in the kitchen, got her apron on,
Spreading gossip on the telephone.
Daughter's in the den listening, too.
Momma, be careful . . . monkey see, monkey do.
Those little eyes are watchin' you,
So don't do something that you can't undo.
Monkey see, monkey do
You might not think it matters,
But it's still just as true.
Little eyes are watchin'.
When they grow up . . . they're gonna be just like you.[1]

Children are dry copies of an original. And the original is their father. Some fathers have two copies. I have three. A guy came up to me in a restaurant last week to say hello. He had been to several of my conferences and he wondered if I would come over and meet his family. I walked over to his table and discovered he didn't have a table. He had three tables and one booth because he and his wife have twelve children. *Twelve!* That was one very impressive family. To see twelve well-behaved children in a restaurant was a direct reflection of the father and mother.

Your children are your copies. You may have one, two, three, or twelve, but they are copies of an original. And the original is Dad.

This thought should strike a certain degree of fear in you if you are a dad. The sheer power of so shaping lives through your fathering is an awesome thing. But you should also realize that it can work to your advantage. God's plan is a remarkable one. How does a man anchor and lead his family for at least the next one hundred years? It's very easy to explain from a technological viewpoint. You simply make copies of yourself and then you fax those copies out to the next two or three generations.

Tommy Bolt was known years ago on the PGA tour for his beautiful swing and legendary temper. He was conducting a golf clinic one afternoon for a group of businesspeople who had paid a lot of dollars to get some tips from Bolt. Bolt was showing them how easy the mechanics of the swing really were, and to demonstrate, he turned to his teenage son and said, "Son, imitate what I do for these gentlemen." His son immediately took his nine-iron and threw it into the lake. That's what you call a copy of the original.

The apostle Paul understood this principle hundreds of years before Chester Carlson. He phrased it like this in 1 Corinthians 4:15–17:

> **For if you were to have countless tutors in Christ, yet you would not have many fathers; for in Christ Jesus I became your father through the gospel.**
>
> **I exhort you therefore, *be imitators of me*.**
>
> **For this reason I have sent to you Timothy, who is my beloved and faithful child in the Lord, and *he will remind you of my ways* which are in Christ, just as I teach everywhere in every church.** (emphasis added)

A copy is an imitation of an original. Paul knew that. And that's why he could send Timothy into a situation that needed leadership. Timothy was a dry copy of Paul. And Paul knew that Timothy would not only do what he had seen in Paul, but he would teach the people to imitate the traits of Paul as well.

Be imitators of me! Do as I do! Talk as I talk! Live as I live!

How many fathers could seriously invite their children to do that? Yet that is precisely what we are supposed to do. We are to provide an original that they can copy and imitate for the rest of their lives. Yogi Berra once said, "If you can't imitate him, don't copy him." That's pretty good advice. And the flip side of that is, "If you can imitate him, copy him." Paul viewed himself as a father to Timothy and to the Christians at Corinth. And he had one piece of advice for them: *Be imitators of me.*

But children have imitated their fathers for thousands of years. When Moses spoke to fathers in the book of Deuteronomy, he also understood this principle. Yes, dads are to teach their children, as we saw in the last chapter. And, yes, they are to teach them on purpose, and they are to teach them as they go. But there is another critical element to the teaching of our children. And that is the fact that we teach the loudest with our lives. Read the words of Moses in Deuteronomy 4:

So watch yourselves carefully, . . . lest you act corruptly and make a graven image. . . .When you become the father of children and children's children and have remained long in the land, and act corruptly, and make an idol in the form of anything, and do that which is evil in the sight of the LORD your God so as to provoke Him to anger, I call heaven and earth to witness against you today, that you shall surely perish quickly from the land where you are going over the Jordan to possess it. You shall not live long on it, but shall be utterly destroyed. (vv. 15–16, 25–26)

The first commandment says, "You shall have no other gods before Me." A dad could teach the first commandment to his kids all day long. He could teach them in the pulpit, in the car, at bedtime. He could teach until he was blue in the face. But if he himself turned around and worshiped other gods, so would his children. Monkey see, monkey do. And here's the tough part. Moses promises that as surely as the rising sun, God's judgment would come upon this man's children. All because their father led them astray.

But, as is usual with God, there is a greater promise to the one who loves and serves Him. What happens when a man lives a godly life before his kids? What happens when he walks his talk? "You shall therefore keep His statutes and His commandments which I command you today, that it may go well with you and with your children after you, and that you may prolong your days in the land which the LORD your God is giving you for all time" (Deut. 4:40 NKJV). This man ensures the blessing of God upon his children for generations to come.

No one is more important in the life of a child than his father. And no one thing is more important to that child than seeing his father's example.

There are many traits that children will copy from the example of their father. But there are three that are of particular importance:

1. Children will copy the original *atmosphere* you set at home.
2. Children will copy your original *attitude* toward their mother.
3. Children will copy your original *approachability*.

CHILDREN COPY YOUR ATMOSPHERE

Some of you are going to read the next two hundred words and think that you've heard this before. That's because I touched on this idea in a previous book. But trust me, I need to say it again.

Every home has an atmosphere. Most fathers don't think about atmosphere, but guys who own restaurants do. Ask any restaurant owner about atmosphere and he will talk for fifteen minutes on how important it is. Now most guys don't care about the atmosphere of a restaurant. All we are concerned with is the food. There's a little joint here in Dallas that serves incredible food. The ulpholstery on the chairs is peeling off and the Formica tabletops are stained from thirty years of use. But you literally have to line up to get in there for lunch. And the line is comprised mostly of men. I'll bet you that 95 percent of that restaurant's customers are men. Do you know why? That place has the atmosphere of a toxic waste site. But guys don't care. The food is incredible. That reminds me of that old joke: "Why are there no restaurants on the moon? There's no atmosphere."

Every once in a while, we men take our wives to nice restaurants. To celebrate an anniversary, for instance. And on a special day like that, we don't want to take our wives to some dive. We want to take them out to a place that has good food and great atmosphere. They call great atmosphere "ambience." Do you know what *ambience* means? I looked it up. It means expensive.

Your home is just like a restaurant. Your home has an atmosphere. But there are only two kinds of atmosphere that a home can have. The atmosphere in your home is either *constructive* or it is *destructive*. If the atmosphere in your home is constructive, then that means your wife and children are built up. If the atmosphere in your home is destructive, it means that your wife and children are torn down.

That's it—constructive or destructive. People built up or people torn down. And there's one more thing: Fathers set the atmosphere of their homes. Most of our wives work very hard on the atmosphere of our homes. But ultimately it is the father who sets the moral and spiritual atmosphere.

Which atmosphere describes your home? Let me ask you a question. What was the atmosphere of the home in which you were raised? Was it constructive? Or was it destructive? Were you built up in your home? Or were you torn down?

The great actor Jimmy Stewart passed away during the writing of this book. He grew up in Indiana, Pennsylvania, and he once recalled what the atmosphere of his home was like. Stewart's father was a devoted Christian, a Scottish Presbyterian, who owned a hardware store. And most of young Jimmy's time, when he was not in school, was spent working at the hardware store. In recalling that hardware store, Stewart said:

> It seemed to me to be the center of the universe. It was a three-story structure full to the rafters with everything needed to build a home, hunt a deer, plant a garden and harvest it, repair a car, or make a scrapbook. I could not conceive of any human need that could not be satisfied in that store. Even after I grew up and moved away and saw larger sights, the store remained with me. But then

> I realized that what was central to my life was not just the store but the man who presided over it—my father.[2]

Jimmy Stewart grew up in an atmosphere where he was built up. He was loved, he was encouraged, and he was disciplined when he needed to be. He knew that his father loved him. When he was leaving to go to war, his dad, choked with emotion, slipped a note into his pocket:

> My dear Jim boy,
>   Soon after you read this letter, you will be on your way to the worst sort of danger. . . . But Jim, I am banking on the enclosed copy of the 91st Psalm. The thing that takes the place of fear and worry is the promise in these words. I am staking my faith in these words. I feel sure that God will lead you through this mad experience . . . I can say no more. I continue only to pray. Goodbye, my dear. God bless you and keep you. I love you more than I can tell you.[3]

E. B. White captured it well when he said, "The time not to become a father is eighteen years before a world war." But as he went off to war, Jimmy Stewart went off knowing he was loved and knowing that his father was praying for him. Jimmy Stewart had a father who set an atmosphere of construction. And because he had been built up by his father in a constructive atmosphere, he could face whatever life would bring him.

Contrast Jimmy Stewart's experience with the experience of J. Paul Getty Jr. His father was the richest man in the world. But he rarely saw his father. Getty Jr., who was raised in California primarily by his mother, would see his father only on the rarest of occasions. When he was in high school, he wrote a very special letter to his father. He had wanted to say some very important things to his dad. The letter came back to him from his father with all of the grammatical and spelling errors marked in red pencil. But there was no personal response from his father. Not one word. In looking back to that experience, he summed it up by saying, "I never got over that."[4]

Never is a strong word. But it was the right word. A father who sets a destructive atmosphere, a father who consistently tears down a child, is going to affect that child for the rest of his life. It is common in homes with destructive atmospheres to hear these kinds of phrases: "Shut up!"; "Can't you do anything right?"; "You will never amount to anything."

You remember that old nursery rhyme:

Sticks and stones may hurt my bones,
But words will never hurt me.

Nothing could be farther from the truth. Kids break bones all the time. Just about every guy reading this, at some point in his childhood, had a cast on his arm or his wrist. You break a bone, you wear a cast for a few weeks, and you get over it. No big deal.

But many of us can still remember the words of our childhood that were aimed our way with intent to maim and kill. How long ago did you hear those words? Twenty, thirty, forty, even fifty years ago? They are still as fresh today as when they first wounded us. And they are especially devastating if those words were uttered by a father.

It's not just the words of a father. Atmosphere is set by the presence of a father. Or lack of presence. Perhaps you've heard of Isadora Duncan. She was a famous dancer who was known for her open immorality. And this was a hundred years ago. She once wrote a letter to George Bernard Shaw suggesting that they together "breed" a child. She was absolutely serious. Her reasoning was that with her body and Shaw's brains they could produce a super-child. Shaw declined by saying,

"But what if the child had my body and your brains?" That's a funny line, but it's a tragic story.

She was not asking Shaw to raise the child or to take responsibility for the child. She would raise the child entirely by herself without a father. There are women doing that today, but a hundred years ago it was beyond the realm of comprehension. What kind of atmosphere would produce a woman like that? What influence did her father have on her? Isadora Duncan was a woman without morals. So what kind of original did she copy?

In her own words, she describes the atmosphere that was provided by the memory of her father:

> As my mother had divorced my father when I was a baby in arms, I had never seen him. Once, when I asked one of my aunts whether I ever had a father, she replied, "Your father was a demon who ruined your mother's life." After that I always imagined him as a demon in a picture book, with horns and tail, and when other children at school spoke of their fathers, I kept silent.[5]

A father sets the atmosphere for his child even when he isn't present. Imagine what a father could do for his children by setting an atmosphere of construction. An atmosphere where children are built up rather than torn down.

One day your children will leave home and establish their own families. And your sons will set the atmosphere of their homes. You obviously want that atmosphere to be constructive. So give them something to copy. Show them how to resolve conflict. Refuse to teach them only to explode and walk away. Show them that conflict doesn't have to destroy a relationship or a family. Show them how to listen, how to express their thoughts and feelings, how to come to constructive resolution. Praise them. Encourage them. Give them a blessing instead of a curse.

Marion Gilbert found out firsthand the power of encouragement. She opened her door one morning to go out and get the newspaper. She was surprised to see a cute little dog sitting on her porch with the newspaper in his mouth. The little pup wagged his tail as she took the paper from him. As a way of saying "thanks," she gave the little dog a couple of doggie biscuits. The next morning she opened the door and there again was the little pup. He had one newspaper in his mouth and seven more spread out on the porch.

It works with dogs and it works with kids. Encouragement is the lifeblood of a secure, happy child.

When the Duke of Wellington, the great military leader who defeated Napoleon at Waterloo, was nearing the end of his life, he was invited to a friend's home for dinner. In the midst of their conversation, the friend asked the Duke, who was known as a demanding leader, what he would do differently if he had life to live over again. The Duke pondered that for a minute and said, "I'd give more praise."

One day your daughters will marry men who will set the atmosphere of their homes. So build up your daughter. Remind her regularly of her value and uniqueness. Give her a model of healthy masculinity. Make her completely secure in your love. Let her know that she is a precious creature to be protected and honored. If a young man enters her life who is from a negative home, she will sense it immediately. If he begins to set a negative tone, warning signals will go off in her head, and she will know that something is wrong! Intuitively, she will know that she is in dangerous territory.

Sons and daughters who come from constructive atmospheres tend not to marry people who are destructive. They simply can't breathe emotionally in an atmosphere of sarcasm and cynicism. It is an atmosphere to which they are not accustomed.

If you set an atmosphere of blessing in your home, you will discover that your house will be like a magnet to your kids. It will be the place that they most want to be, along with all their friends!

And because constructive homes produce constructive children, one day those children will rise up, and in turn, bless you.

CHILDREN COPY YOUR ATTITUDE TOWARD THEIR MOTHER

There is one attitude of a father that seems to impact children more than any other single attitude. And that attitude is your attitude toward your wife. And their mother.

> **You husbands likewise, live with your wives in an understanding way, as with a weaker vessel, since she is a woman; and grant her honor as a fellow heir of the grace of life, so that your prayers may not be hindered.**
> (1 Peter 3:7)

A feminist would find this text troubling. After all, Peter says that wives are weaker vessels. Is that a put-down of women? No, it really isn't a put-down of women. It's simply an acknowledgment of the truth. Men are stronger than women. Women are weaker than men. Unless you're married to an Eastern European Olympic shot-putter who's on steroids, your wife is physically weaker than you. In fact, your wife could be the same height as you, and the same weight as you, and you would still be stronger. That's because God created men with 40 percent more muscle mass than women.

So, saying that a wife is a weaker vessel is simply acknowledging the way that God has created men and women.

When a husband treats his wife in an understanding way and when he grants honor to his wife, he is demonstrating for his children that he respects his wife. He values his wife, he cherishes his wife, he appreciates his wife, and he protects his wife from those who would in any way depreciate her.

I recently came across an article by Doug Wilson in *World Magazine* that oozes with biblical wisdom. Let me give you a few highlights from "Treat Her Like a Lady":

> Let's talk about the beauty of feminine weakness. Difficult as the concept is for some males and many feminists to understand, feminine weakness is not a weakness. No woman should ever be evaluated apart from her creation design, or divinely given purpose. . . . Men tend to evaluate all things according to the sort of criterion best illustrated by football—life is simple and stronger and faster are better. And because life is also a contest, everyone is measured by whether or not he or she is "winning." Unfortunately, more than a few foolish women have been sucked into this mindset. . . . The biblically wise woman laughs at any such attempts to turn women inside out. A woman's station is honored and respected in Scripture and should be honored by all Christians as well. The Fifth Commandment requires that children honor their parents. The father's responsibility is to see that this general commandment is honored in particular applications. One of the most important applications is that of honoring the mother of the home.
>
> A husband should never speak to his wife as though she were one of the children. A condescending attitude is completely out of place. . . . He should take the lead in gratitude. He should lead the family in complimenting her on her meals, on her appearance, and for the work she does in keeping the home running smoothly. He should be saying "thank

you" several times every day, and he should insist that his children learn to follow his example . . . a man who insists on respect and honor for his wife is clearly an honorable man himself. A man rarely stands taller than when he stands for a lady.[6]

Way to hum, Doug. He nailed it. Doug went on in his article to recount that when he was a child, his father taught his sons to avoid three major sins. The three sins were lying, disobedience, and disrespecting your mother. I don't think Doug's father and my father were acquainted. But I can tell you this. They both read the same instruction manual. And I'm sure that they both handed out the same type of consequences for disrespect.

How will your children know that you respect their mother? They will hear you compliment her and praise her on a daily basis. They will hear you say things like, "Guys, you are so lucky to have your mom. She is the glue. Do you know that? She covers the bases so that we can have such a great home!" They will notice that when she talks, you don't just tolerate her until she is finished. You listen intently to what she has to say, because her input is so valuable to you. They will hear you apologize to her when you have been short or ill-tempered. They will watch you open the car door for her (yes, even today in modern feminist America), and help her on with her coat. They will even see you wash the dishes and sometimes make the bed!

"Wait a minute," you may be saying. "Does all this really have to do with honor and respect?" You bet it does! When a man honors his wife, he does more than teach his children about the value of their mother. He makes them happy and secure. Children are genuinely delighted to see their dad honor their mom. They sense that all is well on the home front.

Frederick the Great, king of Prussia, was engaged with his army in a strategic battle at Silesia. He gave orders that all fires and lights were to be put out by a certain hour. He was so concerned that his army's position might be given away that he personally toured the camp that evening to make sure that his order was obeyed. Passing by a row of tents, he saw a light flickering inside one of the tents. He walked in and found a captain, Zietern, completing a letter to his wife. Frederick asked the man if he knew of the order; the man said that he did. He threw himself at Frederick's feet and admitted his guilt. He could not deny his disobedience, he had been caught in the act. Frederick told him to get up and then took the man's quill and dipped it into the ink. He then handed the quill to the captain and said, "Add this postscript to your letter. Tomorrow I shall perish on the gallows." The captain wrote what he was told and was, in fact, executed the following day.

That seems harsh, but Frederick knew that he had to be taken seriously. The captain had endangered every man in the camp by his disobedient act. The Prussian army had to know that there were serious consequences for disobeying an order. This is not a chapter on discipline. That came earlier. But suffice it to say that your children must know from your attitude that there will be no disrespect permitted toward their mother. The consequences of such an act will be significant.

I have a friend who recently bought his seventeen-year-old son a truck. Because his son had made so many good choices in his life, he wanted to encourage and honor him. A few months later, my friend began to notice an attitude problem in his son. His son was beginning to act disrespectfully toward his mother. He developed a cocky spirit, and even though his disrespect was subtle, it was clear to everyone that he didn't feel it was important for a guy his age to be obeying his mother. My friend decided to act swiftly and decisively. Calling his son into his room, he said to him, "Son, you know that I love your mother. But you need to know something else. I also like her and respect her."

"Oh, Dad, I like her and respect her too," his son replied.

"Well, the way you have acted lately, you certainly had most of us fooled. So let me tell you what I am going to do. Up till now, you have made some very wise choices in your life. That's why I gave you that truck. But if I don't see some immediate improvement in your attitude toward your mom, I am going to ask you to hand over the keys to your truck."

Remarkably, his son became a new man. His dad had drawn the line, and he knew that, beyond a shadow of a doubt, his dad would stand by his word. If you instill that kind of respect in your son, the woman that he marries will thank you for the rest of her life. For she has married a man who was taught how to respect a woman.

And what about your daughter? A daughter who sees respect modeled, and also learns to respect her mom, becomes a wise young woman. A son who doesn't respect his own mother simply won't get his foot in the door. He just doesn't measure up to the standard set by the original.

Some of you are divorced. And you may have a situation on your hands where your former wife is constantly putting you down in front of the kids. Let me offer you a tip from 1 Peter 3:9: Don't return insult for insult or evil for evil. If she is tearing you down in front of the children, then you take the high road. Don't fall into that trap. Honor her. If you can't say something nice about her then don't say anything at all.

As your children get older, the truth will become clear to them. And they will figure out who was telling the truth and who wasn't. You take the better way, the narrow way, and God will vindicate you before your children at the right time.

CHILDREN COPY YOUR APPROACHABILITY

Samuel Goldwyn, the founder of the MGM studios, once said to a young associate, "I want you to tell me exactly what you think, even if it costs you your job."

That sort of statement doesn't make a person particularly approachable. Children must have the conviction that their fathers are approachable, and that they can talk to them about anything.

I'm sure that most fathers believe that their children are quick to approach them. But a recent survey in America's most popular teen magazine, *Seventeen,* revealed that only 4.1 percent of the teenage girls in America felt that they could approach their fathers and discuss a serious problem.[7] In other words, ninety-six out of one hundred teenage girls don't feel that their fathers are approachable. That is serious.

A recent *USA Today* poll indicated that when teens are under stress or in a crisis, they turn first to music, second to their friends, and third to TV. Moms came in at number thirty-one and fathers barely showed up at number forty-eight.

When a child hits adolescence, he makes a major decision in life. He decides to do one of two things during his teenage years. He will either go to his peers and, together with his peers, he will critique his parents. Or, he will go to his parents and, together with his parents, he will critique his peers.

Obviously, the superior option is number two. We want our children to come to us, and then together with us, evaluate and critique their peers. But if a child is going to come to his parents, he must feel that they are approachable. And the child who feels that he can approach his father has a tremendous advantage.

So what makes a father approachable?

A Father Who Listens

The story is told of President Franklin Roosevelt, who often had to endure long receiving lines at the White House. He complained that those receptions were so superficial that no one was really listening to anyone else. To prove his point, at the next reception, he murmured to each person who came by to shake his hand, "I murdered my grandmother this morning." The guests smiled and responded, "Isn't that wonderful!" or "Keep up the good work" or "It's such a pleasure to meet you, Mr. President." It was not until the ambassador of Bolivia came through that he found someone who was really listening. The Bolivian ambassador gave the president a slight bow and then said, "I'm sure she had it coming."

When you listen to a child you are subconsciously telling that child that he is important. There is nothing more encouraging to a child, preschooler or teenager, than to have her father's undivided attention when she is speaking to him.

I was a speech communications major in college. I took a ton of speech courses. I still remember a persuasive speaking course that was the best course I ever had in college. It wasn't until years after I graduated with a communications degree that it dawned on me that I never had one course in listening. In communication, someone has to speak. But someone also has to listen. And if the listener and the speaker don't connect, there has been no communication.

When your kids talk, look them squarely in the eye. If they are little toddlers, from time to time get down on a knee so you can listen to them at eye level. They will love you for it. And they will come back for more.

That's certainly what David did. Note how he responds to the Lord who listens:

I love the LORD, because He has heard
My voice and my supplications.

Because He has inclined His ear to me,
Therefore I will call upon Him as long as I live.
(Ps. 116:1–2 NKJV)

When you know that someone is listening, you're going to keep communicating. You're going to keep approaching him. That's exactly what we want our kids to do.

A Father Who Understands

Let me put this on the table. Kids who feel consistently misunderstood by their fathers are not going to approach their fathers. They are going to find someone else to talk to.

You've been misunderstood before, and so have I. It's a lousy experience to have someone misunderstand you. It may be a spouse, it may be a friend, it may be your boss. When people misunderstand you, they misread you. And if they continue to do so, you are not going to have any desire to be around them. Why waste your time?

Your children feel the same way. But when they know they have a dad who understands, or at least wants to understand, well, you won't be able to keep them away.

By the way, your children need a dad who can understand their tears. Sometimes words just don't cut it. The hurt goes too deep. And the only way they can communicate what's on their heart is through tears. Listen to those tears. You don't need words. Hear the tears. Tears communicate. And good dads know how to interpret their meaning. I think Max Lucado explains them best:

> Tears.
>
> Those tiny drops of humanity. Those round, wet balls of fluid that tumble from our eyes, creep down our cheeks, and splash on the floor of our hearts . . . they are miniature messengers, on call twenty-four hours a day to substitute

for crippled words. They drip, drop, and pour from the corner of our souls, carrying with them the deepest emotions that we possess. They tumble down our faces with announcements that range from the most blissful joy to darkest despair.

The principle is simple; when words are most empty, tears are most apt.

What do you do when words won't come? When all the nouns and verbs lay deflated at your feet, with what do you communicate? When even the loftiest statements stumble, what do you do? Are you one of the fortunate who isn't ashamed to let a tear take over? Can you be so happy that your eyes water and your throat swells? Can you be so proud that your pupils blur and your vision mists? And in sorrow, do you let your tears decompress that tight chest and untie that knot in your throat?

Or do you reroute your tears and let them only fall on the inside?

Not many of us are good at showing our feelings, you know. Especially us fellows. Oh, we can yell and curse and smoke, yes sir! But tears? "Save those for the weak-kneed and timid. I've got a world to conquer!"

We would do well, guys, to pause and look at the tearstained faces that appear at the cross . . . the tears of Jesus. They came in the garden. I'm sure they came at the cross. Are they a sign of weakness? Do those stains on his cheeks mean he had no fire in his belly or grit in his gut?

Of course not.

Here's the point. It's not just tears that are the issue, it's what they represent. They represent the heart, the spirit, and the soul of a person. To put a lock and key on your emotions is to bury part of your Christ-likeness.[8]

Children should not be allowed to whine. And they should not be permitted to throw fits or tantrums. But they should be allowed to cry. They should be allowed to communicate with tears. And they should know that those tears will be heard and understood.

David described the Father in these words:

> *[He] is near to the brokenhearted,*
> *And saves those who are crushed in spirit.* (Ps. 34:18)

Make sure that you are near when your kids are broken-hearted. And when their spirits get crushed, be quick to hold them, and to love them, and to comfort them. That's a man's work. That's the work of a father. That's what real men do for their children.

And don't be afraid to shed a few tears yourself now and then. If Jesus could do it, so can you.

I'll guarantee you this. If you treat your children with that kind of understanding and tenderness, when they grow up, they will become a copy of the original. And that's one more godly link in the family chain.

—11—

THREE-PEAT

"Satan rocks the cradle when we sleep at our devotions."

—Joseph Hall

It's tough to win a championship. That's true for football, basketball, baseball, hockey, or any other sport that comes to mind. But it's even tougher to win two in a row. To repeat is quite an accomplishment. But to three-peat is next to impossible.

The first time I remember hearing the term *three-peat* is when the Los Angeles Lakers had just won their second NBA title. Pat Riley had about twelve seconds to enjoy that second championship before a reporter asked him about next year. The reporter wanted to know if they could three-peat.

If a team can three-peat, they are candidates for establishing a sports dynasty.

It's hard to win three championships in a row in any sport. But let me throw out something that's even tougher. It's tough to raise three generations in a row that are committed to Christ. It's not impossible, but it certainly is more difficult than winning some athletic competition. It's flat out tough for a man to anchor his family for one hundred years. It's tough work for a man to follow Christ fully and then see his son embrace the baton of faith with his whole heart, and then eventually pass that baton to the next generation. Often, it's in the hand-off between the second and third generations where the baton of faith gets dropped. Quite frankly, that's why it is so rare to see a father three-peat with his son and grandson.

God wants fathers to anchor their families for the next one hundred years. That's not going to happen by accident. That's not going to happen when a man lives carelessly. But when a man gets serious about following Christ with his whole heart, God desires to pour out His blessing not only on that man, but on his children, and his children's children. So if that's true, *why does it seem to often work out in the opposite way in the Bible*?

If you've ever read through Kings or Chronicles in the Old Testament, then you know what I'm talking about. In Israel and Judah, kingship usually passed from father to son (although there were a few exceptions). And the two books of Kings and the two books of Chronicles tell us the stories of the family chains of the kings of Israel and Judah. As you read through the history, it quickly becomes apparent that it was very unusual for a godly father to produce a godly son to become king.

The story on the kings of Israel is pretty sad. All of the kings of Israel were completely godless men. Of the nineteen kings of Israel, not one of them was a godly man. Not one. What a tragedy. Nineteen kings in Israel and not one of them was a godly man or a godly father. Zero for nineteen. That's what you call a slump. A major slump.

There were nineteen kings who ruled over Judah, and of the nineteen, eight of them could be considered good kings. These eight kings were righteous men who walked with God. But the question is this: How many of these godly kings pulled off a three-peat? Well, before we get to three-peat, let's start with repeat. How many of those godly kings were able to repeat? How many of those godly fathers saw their sons follow in their footsteps? The answer is two.

四方乳品工業（股）公司繳費通知　2009/9/1　印

2009 年 08 月　編號 H0854　　0　路線 G1 0

備註：繳款收據請保留三個月！

姓名 AMBER

電話：22914988　地址台中市水湳路136-20號一放辦公室

四方鮮乳

費用項目小計：

上期	本期	沖銷	應繳	預收餘
$876.0	$0.0	$0.0	$876	$0.0

This brings up a very good question. Why was just one man out of thirty-eight able to produce a godly son who produced a godly son who in turn produced another godly son? Especially when God promised to bless them for generations to come if they would follow Him with their whole hearts.

Bruce Wilkinson explains this principle with a great illustration. Bruce will bring out three chairs and set them across the platform. Each chair stands for one generation. Then he gets three guys from the audience to come up and sit in the chairs. The man in the first chair is saved (father); the man in the second chair is saved (son); the man in the third chair is not saved (grandson).

Or to put it another way, the man in the first chair *has* the works of God (father); the man in the second chair *has heard* about the works of God (son); the man in the third chair *doesn't know* about the works of God (grandson).

This is what tends to happen in family chains. The father will know Christ, the son will know Christ, but the grandson won't. It happened all the time in the Bible and it still happens today. Why did God command the father in Deuteronomy 6 to pass these things on to his son and his grandson? Because if he didn't, his family chain could easily go from godliness to godlessness. And it could very easily happen in *less* than a hundred years.

The following chart makes it easy to see the breakdown that can occur in the three generations:

The First Generation	The Second Generation	The Third Generation
Father	Son	Grandson
Knows God	Knows God	Knows not God
Has the works	Knows about the works	Knows not the works
Serves the Lord	Serves the Lord of their fathers	Serves false gods
First-hand faith	Second-hand faith	No faith at all[1]

It's amazing how quickly a vibrant faith can die in the links that make up a family chain. There is no doubt about it. As you read the Bible, this is what usually occurs in a family. The faith of a father is often erased from the family chain by the time his grandchildren reach adulthood. I don't want that to happen in my family, and neither do you. And that's why God has called us to father with our children and grandchildren in mind. We can't afford to take the short view. Too much is at stake.

The family chains of the kings of Israel and Judah prove that this is a trend of the generations. So what in the world can you do to keep that from happening in your family, and what can I do to keep it from happening in mine?

He was a typical driven young man. He was on the fast track in his chosen profession and very busy juggling a writing schedule with a very long list of speaking commitments. On top of all this, he was spending significant amounts of his time as a youth adviser at his church. By his own count, he once worked seventeen nights straight without being home with his family. His five-year-old daughter would cry as he drove off to work, knowing that she probably wouldn't see her daddy again until the next morning.

It was during this extremely frantic chapter of his life that he received a letter that got his attention. It was a letter from his father. And it was a letter that contained some much needed perspective. One paragraph in particular screamed for his attention as he read these words from his concerned father:

> [Your daughter] . . . is growing up in the wickedest section
> of a world much farther gone into moral decline than the
> world into which you were born. I have observed that the
> greatest delusion is to suppose that our children will be
> devout Christians simply because their parents have been,

or that any of them will enter into the Christian faith in any other way than through their parents' deep travail of prayer and faith. But this prayer demands time, time that cannot be given if it is all signed and conscripted and laid on the altar of career ambition. Failure for you at this point would make mere success in your occupation a very pale and washed-affair, indeed.[2]

The young man on the receiving end of that letter was James Dobson. The words of that letter caused him to sit down and rethink his priorities. And twenty or so years later, he's very glad that he did.

Many of us who are striving to be Christian fathers have benefited from the words of James Dobson Jr. Thank God that James Dobson Jr. listened to the words of James Dobson Sr. That letter was an appeal from a very wise father to a very busy son. It was an appeal to focus on the family. His family. And to his credit, he did.

AIN'T NO MOUNTAIN
HIGH ENOUGH

When you climb Mount Everest, you do it in two climbs. I don't know this from experience, I know it because I read a book by a guy who did it. The first climb is a 120-mile trek that enables a team to acclimatize to the altitude. It's more like an extended hike that gives them a chance to adjust to the weight of the gear and get their wind over a couple of weeks. Even if you're in great shape, taking a 120-mile hike that starts at an altitude of 13,000 feet and goes to 20,000 feet is going to take some adjusting. Then, of course, they establish their base camp and start the final ascent.

In 1988, Jim Hayhurst, along with his twenty-year-old son, Jimmy, was part of the Canadian team that was making the ascent to Everest. As they were trekking across the Himalayas on the first stage of the climb, they had to ford one of the many rivers flowing down the lower part of Everest. That's when Jimmy slipped on a rock and fell into the fast-rushing river. He feverishly twisted and tumbled as the river played with him like a rag doll. He tried to grab on to a rock, but the river was simply moving too fast. Suddenly, he stopped. His backpack had caught on a rock in the middle of the river. And just four feet away, the river tumbled over a cliff and dropped one thousand feet to the valley below.

> I couldn't help him. If I started toward him, I might dislodge another rock, I might change the direction or pressure of the water and he might slip off the rock that was holding him above the waterfall. I had to stand, twenty feet away from my son, and watch him hang at the edge of a 1,000-foot cliff, and I couldn't do a thing to help him. . . . Jimmy slowly reached back, looking for a secure handhold. His hand found only loose rocks, nothing that could support his weight. Then finally he reached to his left and found some rocks that didn't shift when he grasped them. He would be able to put his weight on them. Now he needed a way back upstream.
>
> "Throw me a rope," he called over his shoulder.[3]

And they did. And by the very slim margin of forty-eight inches, he avoided falling a thousand feet to a sure and swift death.

If you are a Christian father, it's your responsibility to throw a rope to the second and third generations. Actually, that's not right. Let me back up and take another shot at it. If you are a Christian father, it's your responsibility to *ask God* to throw a rope to the second, and especially, the third generation. You see, I can't save my future grandchildren and neither can you. But God can. I can't throw a rope to my future grandchildren to save them from the one-thousand-foot fall over the cliff into an eternity without Christ. But God can.

So what part do we play in that process? Somewhere I read that "the effectual, fervent prayer of a righteous man avails much." As a matter of fact I read that in James 5:16 (NKJV). And that's where the prayer of a father plays a critical role. And I do mean critical. I think that's what James Dobson's dad was saying to him in that letter. If you recall, there was a very insightful line in that paragraph: "I have observed that the greatest delusion is to suppose that our children will be devout Christians simply because their parents have been, or that any of them will enter into the Christian faith *in any other way than through their parents' deep travail of prayer and faith*" (emphasis added).

If you want to see your family chain over the next several generations come to Christ, it's going to take more than saying grace before you eat dinner. I wish I could tell you that there is a shortcut. But there isn't. George Mueller knew what it was to stay with the task when it came to praying: "The great fault of the children of the God is, they do not continue in prayer; they do not go on praying; they do not persevere. If they desire anything for God's glory, they should pray until they get it. Oh, how good, and kind, and gracious . . . is the One with Whom we have to do!"[4]

You see, this is what separates the men from the boys. And I also think it is the answer to the dilemma that is presented in looking at the kings of Judah and Israel. Why is it so difficult to three-peat? Why is it that so many third-generation children don't have the faith in Christ that their grandfathers had? Let me shoot absolutely straight. Could it come down to a lack of prayer for that third generation from the first generation? Could it be the first generation just *assumed* that the second and third generations would embrace faith in Christ? That is a severe assumption to make.

There's a big debate going on in Washington, D.C., about how we can ensure that Social Security will be available for the next two or three generations. The real question that Christian fathers should be asking is, How can the second and third generations of my family embrace eternal life through Jesus Christ? Social Security is over for a retired person in twenty to thirty years. And then it's time to face the real question: What is my security status in regard to eternity? Isn't it amazing how many people are fixated on the wrong issue? The central issue is not your Social Security. The central issue is your security for eternity. And the security of at least the next three generations in your family chain.

I want my children, grandchildren, and great-grandchildren to know Christ and to enjoy Him forever. I cannot assume that will happen by accident. As a Christian father I must continually go to the heavenly Father and ask Him to bring each future link in my family chain to Him. Have you ever asked God to save every single one of the next three generations of your family?

If a righteous man consistently goes before the Father and asks Him to save the second and third generations, then do you honestly think that God is going to turn down a consistent thirty- or forty-year prayer from one of His righteous men? I don't think so. That's not how God operates:

> Or what man is there among you, when his son shall ask him for a loaf, will give him a stone? Or if he shall ask for a fish, he will not give him a snake, will he? If you then, being evil, know how to give good gifts to your children, how much more shall your Father who is in heaven give what is good to those who ask Him! (Matt. 7:9–11)

It would be interesting to know, in families where the third generation went astray, if there was a righteous man who consistently and fervently prayed for the third generation. I can't prove this, but I don't think so. James is pretty clear when he says, "You have not because you ask not." C. H. Spurgeon often reminded his congregation that God was serious about His promises to answer prayer:

> I cannot imagine any one of you tantalizing your child by exciting in him a desire that you did not intend to gratify. It would be a very ungenerous thing to offer alms to the poor, and then when they hold out their hand for it, to mock their poverty with a denial. It would be a cruel addition to the miseries of the sick if they were taken to the hospital and there left to die unattended and uncared for. Where God leads you to pray, He means you to receive.[5]

I know that you've prayed for your children to come to faith in Christ. But have you ever prayed for your grandchildren? I mean consistently prayed. How about your great-grandchildren? Somebody needs to pray for those kids. And somebody needs to start praying now. And somebody needs to keep praying.

Thanks to Louis Pasteur, you were able to put cream in your coffee today without worrying about getting sick from the bacteria in the cream. Pasteur was a noted immunologist, and when he was a young scientist thousands of people died each year from rabies. Pasteur had been working for many years on a vaccine and had decided to experiment with the vaccine on himself. But a nine-year-old boy by the name of Joseph Meisner was bitten by a rabid dog, and his hysterical mother convinced Pasteur to try his vaccine on the boy. For ten days, Pasteur gave injections to the young boy. And the boy lived.

Many years later, Pasteur was making preparations for his own death. He was asked what he would like carved on his headstone. Pasteur had accumulated a lifetime of great achievements. But he replied that he only wanted three words for his epitaph: JOSEPH MEISNER LIVED. In telling that story, Wayne Willis made the following observation: "Our greatest legacy will be those who live eternally because of our efforts."[6]

So why don't Christian fathers consistently pray for their children, grandchildren, and great-grandchildren? Perhaps you've heard me say this before but it is worth saying again. The reason that we don't pray is that we don't *plan* to pray. John Piper lays it out for us to ponder:

> Unless I'm badly mistaken, one of the main reasons so many of God's children don't have a significant prayer life is not so much that we don't want to, but that we don't plan to. If you want to take a four-week vacation, you don't just get up one summer morning and say, "Hey, let's go today!" You won't have anything ready. You won't know where to go. Nothing has been planned. But that is how many of us treat prayer. We get up day after day and realize that significant times of prayer should be a part of our life, but nothing's ever ready. We don't know where to go. Nothing has been planned. No time. No place. No procedure. . . . If you want renewal in your life of prayer you must plan to see it.
>
> Therefore, my simple exhortation is this: Let us take time this very day to rethink our priorities and how prayer fits in. Make some new resolve. Try some new venture with God. Set a time. Set a place. Choose a portion of Scripture to guide you. Don't be tyrannized by the press of busy days. We all need mid-course directions.[7]

Allow me to put some more meat in the stew: Christian fathers consistently pray for their children . . . and the wise ones expand their prayers to cover their grandchildren and great-grandchildren.

A couple of hundred years ago in England, there was a young man by the name of James Taylor. This is not the James

Taylor you heard in concert when you were in college. This is another James Taylor. One of his favorite pastimes was to show up wherever John Wesley was preaching. But he didn't show up to listen to him. He showed up to harass him and throw rocks at Wesley while he was preaching in the open air.

One afternoon, as he stood on the edge of a crowd listening to one of Wesley's circuit-riding preachers, he heard these words come out of the preacher's mouth: ". . . as for me and my house, we will serve the LORD" (Josh. 24:15 NKJV). Those words cut him to the quick. The conviction of the Holy Spirit was heavy upon him. Two days later was James Taylor's wedding day. It was on that morning that he could take it no longer. On his way to the wedding, he dropped to his knees and asked Christ to forgive him of his sins.

He got to the chapel just in time for the wedding. At the reception he announced before his friends and family that he had received Christ. And no one was more shocked than his new wife. She looked at him and said, "Have I married one of John Wesley's circuit riders?"[8] Shortly thereafter, his wife came to know Christ. And the next *seven* generations, even to this day, have faithfully followed Christ.

James Taylor had a great-grandson by the name of Hudson Taylor. Hudson Taylor was one of the greatest missionaries in the history of Christianity. In fact, Hudson Taylor is one of the greatest men in the history of Christianity since the apostles. He was the first British missionary to leave the coast of China and head inland to where the vast majority of Chinese people were. God used Hudson Taylor to bring hundreds of thousands of people to Christ.

But at the age of seventeen, Hudson Taylor was not a Christian. Even though his father, his grandfather, and his great-grandfather had left him a great spiritual heritage, he apparently had no interest in following Christ. James Hudson

Taylor III, who represents the eighth generation of the Taylor family to follow Christ, tells what happened to young Hudson Taylor.

> His mother was deeply burdened for him. Once when she was off for a few days to visit friends and relatives, she determined to set aside a particular day to pray for her son. Miles away from home, she knew that he would not be at the bank that day (where he was employed) but would be at home. As she, fasting, knelt that day, she prayed, "Lord, do a new work in my son's heart."
>
> At home, Hudson slipped into his father's study and there saw a gospel tract. He thought, "These tracts always begin with an interesting story. I'll read the story and forget the message. I'm not interested in that." He picked it up. The tract was titled, "The Finished Work of Christ."
>
> He thought to himself, "Why is the author emphasizing the 'finished' work of Christ?" That question motivated him to read the entire tract. As he stood in his father's study it was the message of that small little tract that pierced his heart. And he dropped to his knees and surrendered his life to Christ.[9]

Three generations before Hudson Taylor followed Christ with their whole hearts. And four generations since Hudson Taylor have followed Christ with their whole hearts. Why has God blessed the Taylor family in such a remarkable way for *eight* generations? Is there something here in the Taylor family chain that gives us a clue? I think that there is.

CONSISTENT PRAYER, OCCASIONAL FASTING

When Hudson Taylor's mother went off by herself to be alone with God, she did two things. She obviously prayed.

But there was something else that she did. She not only prayed, but she fasted. And I seriously doubt that she was the only person in the Taylor family chain to ever do so. Eight generations of strong believers do not just naturally come about. Eight generations of committed Christian families are the result of more than one person praying and fasting for God's favor on their family.

At a critical point in World War II, General George Patton received word from one of his commanders that his troops were holding their ground. He shot back a reply: "I don't want to hear that you're holding your ground. I'm not interested in holding ground. I'm interested in taking ground."

If we are serious about taking ground for our families over the next one hundred years, then we are going to have to put ourselves on the line. We are going to have to go beyond the normal. We are going to have to go the extra mile.

Jesus made a significant point on fasting in Matthew 6:16–18:

> **And whenever you fast, do not put on a gloomy face as the hypocrites do, for they neglect their appearance in order to be seen fasting by men. Truly I say to you, they have their reward in full. But you, when you fast, anoint your head, and wash your face so that you may not be seen fasting by men, but by your Father who is in secret; and your Father who sees in secret will repay you.**

Jesus made quite a few points but I want to camp on just one of them. Notice that Jesus didn't say "if" you fast. He said "when" you fast. He assumed that fasting was something that His disciples would do from time to time. But fasting has become a lost art. I believe that the father who considers occasional fasting for his children, along with consistent prayer, will see God do great things in response to his obedience.

There is usually a cost to taking ground. Taking ground is going to cost someone something. When it comes to spiritually leading a family, most Christian men are just holding ground. But if your children, your grandchildren, and your great-grandchildren are going to know Christ personally, then you can't be content to just hold your ground. If the next three or four generations of your family are going to follow Christ seriously, then you are going to have to not just hold your ground, you're going to have to take some ground. If your grandchildren are going to know Christ, somebody better start praying and fasting for those kids. If your children, and your grandchildren, and your great-grandchildren are going to love the Lord their God with all their heart, with all their mind, and with all their soul, somebody better start taking some ground . . . and that somebody is you. You're the father, and you are the anchor for your family chain.

FAST FOOD

You may be thinking, *Hey, I'm willing to pray for my kids, but what's this fasting jazz? I'm not a spiritual giant, I'm just an average guy. I can pray but I'm not sure I can get into this fasting business.* Sure you can. Do you know what it means to fast? It simply means that instead of eating a meal, you take the time that would be devoted to the meal and you pray. That's it.

If fasting is so important, then how come we don't hear more about it? That's a very good question. There is no question that fasting is important in the Scriptures. Most Christians would not deny that baptism is an important Christian teaching. But do you realize that fasting is mentioned in the Scriptures approximately seventy-seven times and baptism is referred to seventy-five times?[10] That makes me think that fasting is fairly critical. But fasting has become a lost art.

One of the reasons that fasting isn't focused on a whole lot is that fasting is a discipline. Fasting can be hard. But it yields great dividends.

Unless you have a health issue in your life, instead of eating lunch at work, you could probably just shut the door of your office and spend your thirty-minute lunchtime reading the Word and praying for the next three generations of your family. Or four. Or five.

Jesus fasted for forty days. So did Moses. You don't have to fast for forty days for God to hear your prayer. All you have to do is start maybe with fasting one meal. Or maybe you want to fast for one day. The length of fast is not the issue. Your heart is the issue. But guys, the point is this. If we are serious about seeing our families follow Christ for the long haul, we are going to have to take some ground.

- When Moses needed to take some ground, he prayed and fasted.
- When Jehoshaphat needed to take some ground, he prayed and fasted.
- When Josiah needed to take some ground, he prayed and fasted.
- When Daniel needed to take some ground, he prayed and fasted.
- When Ezra needed to take some ground, he prayed and fasted.
- When Nehemiah needed to take some ground, he prayed and fasted.
- When Mordecai and Esther needed to take some ground, they prayed and fasted.
- When Joel needed to take some ground, he prayed and fasted.
- When Paul and Barnabas, and the elders at Antioch, needed to take some ground, they prayed and fasted.

When you want to take some ground, what do you do?

All of these people in the Bible were facing different situations. Some of them were at war, some of them faced extermination, some of them needed guidance, some of them needed wisdom. But they did have something in common: In their different situations they all realized that if God did not directly intervene on their behalf, there was absolutely *no hope* for a solution. That's what I mean by taking ground. They knew that they couldn't advance if God did not do it for them. The need was too great and the circumstances were too severe . . . it was absolutely beyond their abilities to accomplish what they needed to accomplish. Only God could do it. That's why they prayed and fasted.

When a father fasts and prays for his children and grandchildren, he is acknowledging that those children are beyond his reach. He is acknowledging that only God can do the work in the hearts of his children and grandchildren that will bring them to Christ. Let me ask you something. Is there anything that you can think of that is more important than your children, grandchildren, and great-grandchildren knowing Christ?

Then why not make it a priority on a regular basis—once a week, once a month, once a quarter, or once every six months, to pray and fast for the salvation of those who will follow you in your family chain? Fathers can spend their time doing hundreds of activities and tasks with their kids. It would be tragic to attend all the games and coach the teams and show up for dance recitals and band concerts and miss the most important work of a father.

During World War II, President Franklin Roosevelt's most trusted adviser was a man by the name of Harry Hopkins. Roosevelt trusted Hopkins as he trusted no one else. But Hopkins was dying. He knew it and everyone around him knew it. Peter Drucker describes the situation:

A dying, indeed almost a dead man for whom every step was torment, he could only work a few hours every other day or so. This forced him to cut out everything but truly vital matters. He did not lose effectiveness thereby; on the contrary, he became, as Churchill called him once, "Lord Heart of the Matter" and accomplished more than anyone else in wartime Washington.[11]

How could a man who could only work ten to twelve hours a week get more done than men who were putting in eighty hours a week? Hopkins did it by focusing on the heart of the matter. He did it by focusing on the few things that were truly important. That's what fasting does. It helps you to get to the heart of the matter as a concerned father.

One word of caution. Fasting is not a gimmick. Fasting is not a spiritual slot machine. Fasting is not a way of getting God to do what we want. Fasting is not a method of spiritual manipulation. Fasting is a spiritual discipline that enables us to get closer to the Father and discover what He wants. When we fast we are not manipulating God, we are *humbling ourselves* before Him. In that spirit of humility, we are asking Him to graciously consider our request that He would supernaturally work in the lives of our children, grandchildren, and great-grandchildren.

There's nothing more important than a father setting aside time on a regular basis and consistently praying and occasionally fasting for his children and their children. But you may be thinking, *I'm so busy already, how will I fit in time to pray?*

Do you jog? Then talk to God about your children when you're jogging. Do you walk? Then use your walking time to pray. Do you commute? Then turn off the radio for fifteen minutes or so on your way to the office and talk to the Lord. I talk to the Lord all the time in my car. And I often do it out loud. People driving by used to look at me sometimes as though I were nuts. But I've noticed that in the last couple of years, hardly anyone ever looks at me when I'm talking by myself in my car. They assume that I'm making a call on my speakerphone.

The point is this: You already have time in your schedule to pray. You simply have to schedule it in. And fasting is no sweat. You've got a lunch hour, right? Well, just make a plan to not eat during lunch. Drink a Gatorade, or a Slim-Fast, and use the time you would normally take for lunch to sit at your desk, or in your car, or at a park, and have some time with the Lord. Crack open your Bible and pray specifically!

There is a key to fasting and this is it: *Whenever you fast you should do so with a set purpose in mind*. Every time someone in the Scriptures fasted they did so with a specific purpose. Without a purpose, fasting is drudgery and miserable. But with a purpose, it sharpens our prayers and hones the edge of our faith to a razor-sharp edge. So what is one of the most important responsibilities of Christian fatherhood? It is to pray and fast for the salvation of my children and grandchildren so that they might fear the Lord and that Deuteronomy 6:1–2 would be fulfilled in my family chain.

So what do you pray about? Here are a few ideas:

- Pray that your kids would truly come to know Christ as their Lord and Savior.
- Pray for your son's future wife. And pray for your daughter's future husband. "But I don't know who they will marry!" That's right, you don't. But God does.
- Pray for the husband and wife who are raising the child that will marry your child. Pray that they will follow Christ with their whole hearts. Pray that the husband will love his wife as Christ loves the church. Pray that divorce will not hit their family. Pray that the father and mother will model sexual purity for their family.

- Pray for your son or daughter who isn't walking with Christ. Pray and *fast* that God will change your child's heart and bring him or her home.

That ought to get you started. And you'll think of a number of other things to pray about once you get rolling. But there's one other specific request that you should consider bringing to the Lord. Pray that your children, grandchildren, and great-grandchildren will *experience* firsthand the work of God in their lives. A lot of people know about Jesus Christ. But there is a world of difference between knowing about Christ and knowing Christ.

So how do you go about fasting if you've never done it?

- You can fast for a meal.
- You can fast for a day.
- You can do a Daniel fast (just vegetables and water as in Dan. 1:12).

After James Dobson got that letter from his dad, he started to consistently pray for the salvation of his children. But he didn't stop there. He started to fast every Tuesday for the salvation of his children.

Over the last ten years, I have made sure that I have set aside times of fasting for my children. And it has paid off. I'll be honest with you. One of the reasons I fast is that I want to three-peat. Actually I want to do more than that. I'd like for God to do for me what He did for James Taylor. You see, I represent the third generation in my family that is following Christ. And I'd like to see God give us at least five more generations. How many generations would you like God to give to you?

But don't I think that Christ is coming back soon? Why should I be concerned for the next five generations if Christ is going to come back quickly? Let me shoot straight with you. Christ may come tomorrow afternoon or He may come back in five hundred years. I hope He comes back tomorrow, but I must occupy *until* He comes. I'm sure not going to assume that I have the inside track on knowing when He is coming back.

So in the interim, I'm going to ask Him to bring each generation of my family chain to know Him until He comes. When Christ returns is the Father's business. Consistently praying and occasionally fasting for the coming generations is my business. And if we don't pray for the next two or three generations in our family chains, then who will?

I'll be honest with you. There are few Christian fathers who have the vision to pray for the next three or four generations of their family chain. And there are few Christian fathers who will occasionally fast for a day on behalf of their children. The Christian fathers who do this for their children are going the extra mile. And there's plenty of room for you to join them. For there is very little traffic on the extra mile.

Hans Bret went the extra mile. Hans Bret was not a father. He was burned at the stake in 1577 at the age of twenty-one before he had the opportunity to marry and have a family. But I want to tell you about Hans Bret because he three-peated for his family in a unique way.

At the age of twenty-one, Hans Bret was working in a bakery to support his widowed mother. But he spent every free moment preaching the gospel in the Netherlands. He was having such an impact that one day the authorities came to his house and arrested him. He was taken to a castle in Antwerp where he was tortured for several months because he refused to compromise his faith in the teachings of the

Scriptures. Then he was thrown into a dungeon for several weeks.

He was then tortured again, but he refused to recant. Finally, he was put on trial and when given the opportunity to speak, he preached a powerful message to all in the courtroom about the power of the gospel of Jesus Christ. The exasperated judge found him guilty and sentenced him to be burned at the stake.

> Early in the morning of the day set for the burning, Saturday, 4 January, the executioner came to Hans's cell. The executioner ordered him to put out his tongue. Over it he placed an iron clamp, then screwed it tight with a vice-screw over the tongue. This done, he burned the end of Hans's tongue with a hot iron so that the tongue would swell and could not be withdrawn from the clamp.[12]

Why in the world did the authorities clamp and burn the tongue of this young preacher? Because they knew if they didn't, on his way to the stake he would use his tongue to preach the gospel to the crowds who had gathered to watch him die.

As Hans was chained to the stake to be burned, his close friend and mentor, Hans de Ries, got as near to the young man as he could. He watched the young man die in the flames for his faith. Hours later, after the body was nothing but ashes and the coals had cooled, Hans de Ries found the only item that had survived the intense heat of the flames. He reached down into the soot and pulled out the tongue screw.

A short time later, Hans de Ries married Hans Bret's widowed mother. And a unique tradition began. For more than three hundred years, the tongue screw that was used to silence Hans Bret has been handed down from one generation to the next. It is still in his family to this day. That's what you call a three-peat. A three-hundred-year three-peat.

And it is living proof that it is impossible to silence the message of a man who is serious about following Christ with everything he has.

NOTES

Chapter 1

1. Perspectives, *Newsweek,* 9 September 1996, 25.
2. R. Marin, interview with Howard Stern, in *Rolling Stone,* 10 February 1994, 28–53, cited by Chapman Reynolds Clark, "Adolescent Son and Daughter Sibling Perceptions of Their Attachment Relationships with Their Father," Doctoral Dissertation, Univ. of Denver, June 1996, p. 1.
3. Ron Blue, *How to Determine Your Investment Strategy* (Ronald Blue & Co., 1100 Johnson Ferry Rd., N.E., Suite 800, Atlanta, GA 30342), 16.
4. Ray Stedman, *Family Life* (Waco: Word, 1973), 56–57.
5. Crawford Loritts, *Never Walk Away* (Chicago: Moody, 1997).

Chapter 2

1. J. Allen Petersen, *Family Building,* ed. Dr. George Rekers (Ventura, Calif.: Regal Books, 1985), 104.
2. Ibid., 105.
3. David Blankenhorn, *Fatherless America* (New York: Basic Books, 1995), 1.
4. David Popenoe, *Life Without Father* (New York: Free Press, 1996), 192.
5. James C. Dobson, *Straight Talk to Men and Their Wives* (Waco: Word, 1980), 21.
6. Position Paper on Divorce Reform, Frequently Asked Questions (Family Research Council, 700 Thirteenth St., N.W., Suite 500, Washington, DC 20005), 8.
7. Interview with Dr. Wade Horn, National Fatherhood Initiative, *Men's Health,* September 1995, 48.
8. Popenoe, *Life Without Father,* 22.
9. Ibid., 192.
10. Quoted in Position Paper on Divorce Reform, 2.

Chapter 3

1. Carlo D'Este, *Patton: A Genius for War* (New York: HarperCollins, 1995), 9.
2. Ibid., 11.
3. Ibid., 12.

4. Ibid., 12.
5. Ibid.
6. Ibid., 15.
7. Gordon MacDonald, *The Effective Father* (Wheaton, Ill.: Tyndale, 1977), 18.
8. Quoted in Samuel Osherson, *Finding Our Fathers* (New York: Fawcett Columbine, 1986), 55.
9. I think that I first heard "speed-model" from Bobb Biehl, president of Masterplanning Group. Bobb has some great materials on leadership. He can be reached at Masterplanning Group, P.O. Box 952499, Lake Mary, FL 32795, or call (407) 330-2028.
10. Daniel G. Reid, *Dictionary of Christianity in America, Puritanism* (Downers Grove, Ill.: InterVarsity, 1990), 966.
11. Ibid.
12. Popenoe, *Life Without Father,* 88.
13. Ibid., 89–90.
14. Ibid., 90.
15. Blankenhorn, *Fatherless America,* 12–13.
16. Popenoe, *Life Without Father,* 96–97.
17. Ibid., 96.

Chapter 4

1. Josh McDowell, *Right From Wrong* (Dallas: Word, 1994), 8.
2. Ibid., 13.
3. Ibid., 16.
4. Ralph G. Martin, *Seeds of Destruction* (New York: Putnam, 1995), xvii.
5. Ibid., xx.
6. C. F. Keil and F. Delitzsch, *Commentary on the Old Testament,* vol. I, *The Pentateuch* (Grand Rapids: Eerdmans, 1980), 323.
7. Henry T. Blackaby and Claude V. King, *Experiencing God* (Nashville: Lifeway Press, 1990), 27.
8. *Family News* from Dr. James Dobson, November 1996, Focus on the Family, p. 1.
9. Alice Gray, *Stories for the Heart* (Sisters, Oreg.: Multnomah, 1996), 79.
10. Ibid.
11. Ibid.
12. Ibid., 205.
13. Martin, *Seeds of Destruction*, 23.

Chapter 5

1. Charlie Hedges, *Getting the Right Things Right* (Sisters, Oreg.: Multnomah, 1996), 171.

2. *The Washington Times,* National Weekly Edition, August 25, 1996, 21.
3. William Beausay II, *Boys!* (Nashville: Thomas Nelson, 1994), 23.
4. Quoted in Petersen, *Family Building,* 54.
5. Ibid., 52.
6. Norman Rose, *Churchill: The Unruly Giant* (New York: Free Press, 1994), 14.
7. Beausay, *Boys!,* 47.

Chapter 6

1. National & International Religion Report, March 18, 1996, vol. 10, no. 7, 1.
2. *U.S. News and World Report,* 25 March 1996, 68.
3. John J. Dilulio, "Kids Who Scare Cops; Focus on the Family," *Citizen,* vol. 10, no. 1, 15 January 1996, 10.
4. Andrew Peyton Thomas, *Crime and the Sacking of America* (Washington, D.C.: Brassey's Inc., 1994), xxiv.
5. Dan Korem, "Youth Gangs," *Dallas Morning News,* 14 January 1996, 6-J.
6. Issues '96: The Candidate's Briefing Book, Heritage Foundation, chap. 6, 2.
7. Charles R. Swindoll, *Strengthening Your Grip* (Waco: Word, 1982), 265.
8. Charles R. Swindoll, *You and Your Child* (Nashville: Thomas Nelson, 1977), 64.
9. Dr. James Dobson, "Discipline from Four to Twelve," Focus on the Family Booklet, 16–17.
10. "Spare the Rod," in Family Policy, Family Research Council, October 1996, vol. 9, no. 5, 3.
11. Ibid., 4.
12. R. Laird Harris, Gleason L. Archer, and Bruce K. Waltke, *Theological Wordbook of the Old Testament* (Chicago: Moody, 1980), 897.
13. Ibid.
14. Swindoll, *You and Your Child,* 91–92.

Chapter 7

1. Charles R. Swindoll, *The Strong Family* (Portland, Oreg.: Multnomah, 1991), 61.
2. Thomas Armstrong, *Seven Kinds of Smart* (New York: Plume Books, 1993), 9.
3. Swindoll, *You and Your Child,* 27.

4. Ibid., 21.
5. Arthur F. Miller and Ralph T. Mattson, *The Truth About You* (Old Tappan, N.J.: Revell, 1972), 9.
6. Hedges, *Getting the Right Things Right,* 73.
7. Miller and Mattson, *The Truth About You,* 15–17.
8. Donald O. Clifton and Paula Nelson, *Soar with Your Strengths* (New York: Delacorte Press, 1992), 3.
9. Bobb Biehl, *Weathering the Midlife Storm* (Wheaton, Ill.: Victor Books, 1996), 138.
10. Ibid., 139–41.
11. Clifton and Nelson, *Soar with Your Strengths,* 19.

Chapter 8
1. Charles R. Swindoll, *The Finishing Touch* (Dallas: Word, 1994), 222.
2. Geraldine Fabrikant, "Patricia Cornwell: New Chapter for a Serial Spender," *New York Times,* 23 March 1997, Money & Business, sect. 3, 1.
3. *Encyclopaedia Britannica,* 34th ed., s.v. "Sir William Wallace."
4. John Piper, *Future Grace* (Sisters, Oreg.: Multnomah, 1995), 330–31.
5. Donald E. Wildmon, Freedom, March–April 1997, devotional prayer pamphlet published by the American Family Association, 107 Parkgate, P.O. Drawer 2440, Tupelo, MS 38803.

Chapter 9
1. Francis A. Schaeffer, *Joshua and the Flow of Biblical History* (Downers Grove, Ill.: InterVarsity, 1975), 87.
2. Gray, *Stories for the Heart,* 168.
3. Franklin Graham, *Rebel with a Cause* (Nashville: Thomas Nelson, 1995), 98.

Chapter 10
1. Brent Lamb and Paul Guffey, "Monkey See, Monkey Do." Copyright 1994 Paul Guffey Music/ASCAP (administered by CMI) and Van Ness Press, Inc./ ASCAP (a div. Of GMG).
2. "Nice Guys Finish First in the Hearts of Their Countrymen," *The American Spectator,* December 1996, vol. 29, no. 12, 78.
3. Ibid., 79.
4. Alexandra Towle, *Fathers* (New York: Simon and Schuster, 1986), 222.
5. Ibid., 114.

6. Douglas Wilson, "Treat Her Like a Lady," *World Magazine,* 7 September 1996, 26.
7. *Homemade,* November 1989.
8. Max Lucado, *No Wonder They Call Him the Savior* (Sisters, Oreg.: Multnomah, 1986), 50.

Chapter 11

1. Bruce Wilkinson, *First-Hand Faith* (Portland, Oreg.: Vision House, 1996), 22.
2. James Dobson, *Straight Talk to Men and Their Wives* (Waco: Word, 1980), 49.
3. Jim Hayhurst Sr., *The Right Mountain* (Toronto: John Wiley & Sons, 1996), 97–98.
4. Donald S. Whitney, *Spiritual Disciplines for the Christian Life* (Colorado Springs: NavPress), 77.
5. Ibid., 75.
6. *Leadership Journal,* vol. XVII, no. 3, Summer 1996, 64.
7. John Piper, *Desiring God* (Portland, Oreg.: Multnomah, 1986), 150.
8. James Hudson Taylor III, "Four Spiritual Principles Illustrated in Eight Generations of One Family," *Bryan Life Magazine,* Spring 1985, 6.
9. Ibid., 7.
10. Whitney, *Spiritual Disciplines for the Christian Life,* 152.
11. Peter Drucker, *The Effective Executive* (New York: Harper and Row, 1966), 40.
12. "The Story of Hans Bret," *Christian History*, vol. IV, no. 1, 28.

STEVE FARRAR
In Person
In Your City